GRUDGE MATCH

GRUDGE MATCH

Are You Ready to Rumble?

Brian Wright & Steve Levine

HarperPerennial

A Division of HarperCollinsPublishers

This book was not prepared, approved, licensed, endorsed, marketed, or used to prop up their sofa by any person, company, religion, cult, government agency, political party, or auto club we poked fun at. Any resemblance to real persons, living or dead, was pretty much the point. Jokes not funny in Alaska, Hawaii, or where prohibited by law.

Photos courtesy of Photofest. Boris Yeltsin photo (p. 89) courtesy of AP/Wide World Photos. Line art by Jim Houghton.

HarperCollins books may be purchased for educational, business, or sales promotional use. For information please write: Special Markets Department, HarperCollins Publishers, Inc., 10 East 53rd Street, New York, NY 10022.

FIRST EDITION

Designed by Elina D. Nudelman

Library of Congress Cataloging-in-Publication Data
Wright, Brian, 1972–
    Grudge match : are you ready to rumble? / Brian Wright & Steve Levine.—1st ed.
      p.   cm.
    ISBN 0-06-095264-4
    1. American wit and humor.   I. Levine, Steve, 1971–   .
    II. Title.
PN6162.W75   1998   97-51585
818'.5407—dc21

98 99 00 01 02 ❖/RRD 10 9 8 7 6 5 4 3 2 1

*To the film and network TV executives,
past and present, for supplying us with the
consistently bad entertainment that made
something like this inevitable.*

And to Aaron Spelling.

Contents

Introduction   **ix**

THE MATCHES

Forrest Gump vs. Rain Man   **1**

Dennis Rodman vs. RuPaul   **8**

Gary Coleman vs. Webster   **14**

Pee-wee Herman vs. Gilligan   **19**

Flipper vs. Jaws   **25**

The Bandit vs. CHiPs   **30**

Rush Limbaugh vs. Howard Stern   **36**

Mr. T vs. Mr. Clean   **43**

A Rottweiler vs. A Rottweiler's Weight in Chihuahuas   **49**

The Six Million Dollar Man vs. Robocop   **56**

Microsoft vs. Disney   **63**

Colonel Sanders vs. Orville Redenbacher   **70**

Mr. Peanut vs. Poppin' Fresh **77**

KITT vs. Herbie **83**

Boris Yeltsin vs. Ted Kennedy **89**

John McClane vs. The Death Star **97**

ALF vs. E.T. **104**

Scooby-Doo vs. *The X-Files* **110**

Ellen Ripley vs. Sarah Connor **119**

Waldo vs. Carmen Sandiego **126**

Andy Taylor vs. The Cunninghams **136**

James Bond vs. Indiana Jones **145**

The Brady Bunch vs. The Partridge Family **153**

Pinky & The Brain vs. Dogbert **160**

Rocky vs. Rambo **169**

The Grudge Match™ Panel™ **176**

Appendix A **178**

Acknowledgments **179**

Introduction

How this book came to be:

In ages past, Steve and Brian had a vision, a vision in the form of Mr. T. And he did say, "Hey sucka! You have a gift! Use it to create the funniest Web page on the Internet. Encourage readers to send in responses and match ideas so that it can thrive and prosper. Then, once you have enough material, turn it into a best-selling book and retire to Hollywood. I pity the fool who don't do as I say." So Steve and Brian went forth to create the WWWF Grudge Match, an award-winning Web page which was consistently funny and always errer-free. In the beginning, they created *Gary Coleman v. Webster,* which begat *Pee-wee v. Gilligan,* which begat *Flipper v. Jaws,* which begat *Forrest Gump v. Rain Man.* As foretold in the prophetic vision, the readership grew steadily, and the readers did send in their humorous responses and their new match ideas, and the Grudge Match did prosper. When the time came to publish, many publishers did woo Steve and Brian. And the book you now hold had come to be, as was planned from the very beginning. And so it was written.

How this book *really* came to be:

Okay, so it was late one night about three years ago. Steve, Brian, and their friend Sam were sitting around, pretty bored, and they started talking. As such conversations are likely to do with them, especially when they've had a few, the topic turned to an informal contest as to who could spew out the most irrelevant and obscure TV and movie references. Soon they were arguing over who would win a cage match between the Incredible Hulk and Hulk Hogan or a mud-wrestling match between Wonder Woman and the Bionic Woman. Such topics would resurface occasionally for several weeks, and then Steve had a thought. "We could do something with this. We could turn it into a TV show on public access." But then, in his infinite laziness, he realized that a Web page would be much easier. Thus, after a riveting "I'll do it if you do it" discourse with Brian, *Gary Coleman v. Webster* was born.

Steve and Brian slapped together some comments and threw it up on the Web. A simple voting system allowed Internet surfers to choose the winner. They had hoped to get at least fifty votes. They received fifteen hundred (over eight hundred from a single deranged Gary Coleman fan).

And, surprisingly, people actually sent in their thoughts on who would win this street fight. So after securing the voting system, they wrote another match, and then another. And then, much to their surprise, people started sending in ideas for new matches. Good ones even. Thus, they had an ever increasing pool of ideas to work with. With word of mouth and newsgroup posts, the page grew. One day, Steve and Brian stuck in a "™" where it was completely inappropriate, just to be silly. It quickly caught on, and soon became as ubiquitous as Michael Jordan. After about a year, they received a small but prominent mention in *Entertainment Weekly*, and the hits continued to increase. One of those hits came about six months later from an editor at HarperCollins. He asked if they'd consider turning it into a book. They said yes.

. . . And those two young graduate students . . . otherwise destined to lead boring lives . . . unknown to the world . . . ended up with this book . . . a book which propelled them into stardom. . . . You know these two young men as . . . Steve and Brian. . . . And now you know . . . the Rest of the Story.

ANATOMY OF A GRUDGE MATCH

The Setting — Here is where we lay down the ground rules for the match. The purpose of this section is to introduce the competitors and in what manner they will be competing.

The Commentary — Brian and Steve discuss, debate, and banter on and on about the match. The purpose of The Commentary is to completely cloud the issue by arguing about as many irrelevant and off-topic subjects as possible.

The Outcome — Who won the match, as determined by actual votes from our Web page. Use this as a guide to compare your opinion with that of the masses.

The Peanut Gallery™ — Select responses from our Internet readers. Beware! This is highly concentrated humor. If you read too much at one sitting, dilute with a glass of water or milk and consult a physician immediately.

Forrest Gump vs. Rain Man

THE SETTING

It's a warm, sunny day in Americana, USA. Just outside town at one end of an open field stands a single, modest card table. Seated there are our two contestants; both appear distant and distracted, but ready for action. When the starting gun is fired, our two contestants must complete a 10×10 multiplication table and then run a hundred-yard dash to the other end of the field. The first one across the finish line wins. Judging the event will be the esteemed Vic Tayback. His decisions are final. Who will win?

THE COMMENTARY

BRIAN: I find this match-up extremely fascinating. On the one hand, you have Rain Man's superior mathematical abilities coupled with his inability to walk straight; on the other hand, you have the moronic Forrest Gump with blazing speed. So one can envision Gump forever sitting with that dumb look on his face and Raymond, long since done with the table, wandering in circles saying "Kmart sucks." And then to top it all off you have some guy named Mel judging the whole thing. Well, as athletes of biathlons, triathlons, decathlons, et cetera all know, you're only as strong as your weakest event. And simply put, while it may take forever for Rain Man to make those hundred yards, Gump ain't ever going to get that multiplication table done. Rain Man's speed can also be dramatically increased by strategically placing Tom Cruise in the stands with cardboard cutouts of Judge Wapner and/or Vanna White to be revealed after Raymond finishes the table. It's a done deal—Gump never gets off his chair.

Another note: The result is actually decided by crowd response. Vic cannot make the call as he is blinded by his own plaid jacket.

STEVE: You make some valid points, but I'm going to have to go with Gump on this one. Rain Man will suddenly get the idea that he wants to go driving (after all, he is a great driver) and refuse to fill in the multiplication table until his demands are met. Meanwhile, Forrest will diligently count on his fingers and toes and fill in the multiplication table. Of course, the sprint is nothing to him, and he will finish with Raymond still sitting at the table, pouting, and rocking back and forth in a catatonic state.

You see, Forrest has heart. You can't beat that. He may be

dumb, but dammit, he gives it all he's got. Gump in forty-five minutes.

BRIAN: I'm sorry, Steve, but last time I tried to multiply with my fingers and toes, I couldn't get much past four times five. I got to three times seven one time, but I was naked. Gump just can't pull this off in any reasonable amount of time. Not to say Gump isn't without his skills: Forrest would be great at a chocolate-judging contest, and for successful navigation of a reflecting pool, Gump's your man. But counting and calculating just aren't his strong points. Raymond will be able to fill in the table so quickly that he won't even realize he's missing *Wheel—of—For—tune*. (Remember how quickly he counted those toothpicks? I think my point is made.) Besides, with a little coaching from brother Charlie, Raymond knows that he gets to go driving if he wins the event. (Remember that he probably didn't want to count cards either, but Charlie pulled him through!)

Yes, I agree that Forrest has heart. No one questions that. He has more heart than the 1980 U.S. Olympic Hockey Team. But he's an idiot. No matter how big his heart is, it ain't gonna make his brain any bigger. And besides, while Forrest has heart, Raymond has a more powerful weapon: the Rage™. It will pull him through. (For those of you doubting that Rain Man has rage, I refer you to the "Hot water hurt baby" scene. Frightening.)

STEVE: Only a fool would think that "the Rage™" is going to allow Raymond to do math problems faster. If anything, it will slow him down and confuse him. He's just not good with emotions.

Another advantage Gump may have is the fact that ol' Vic is judge. He probably can't multiply either, and won't know that seven times seven really isn't thirteen. In addition (no pun intended), I don't think Vic will have much patience with Raymond's moody nature, and will probably beat him up just for fun. If Vera annoyed him, what do you think someone like Raymond would make him do?

BRIAN: I think you're vastly misjudging Vic, Steve. Sure he plays a dumb oaf on TV all the time, but Vic himself is actually a pretty bright guy (let's not forget how intelligent Christopher Lloyd and John Cleese are). Plus, going by Vic's build, I'm thinking he played ball, probably offensive line. And while those wiry speedy types might impress The Bear™, they really grate on the boys in the trenches. If anyone is gettin' his butt kicked, it's Gump-boy.

Also, only a fool would think I was saying that rage would make Raymond do the math problems faster. All I said is that rage will focus him to concentrate on what is at hand in the heat of battle. Raymond in 4.3 minutes. Forrest dug his own grave: "I'm not a smart man." End of story.

THE OUTCOME

Forrest Gump (51%) defeats Rain Man (49%).

THE PEANUT GALLERY™

Rain Man takes an early lead, completing the multiplication table in 2.1 seconds, and totters off toward the other end of the field. Meanwhile, Forrest has discovered that poking the sharp end of the pencil into his own flesh hurts, and that . . . wow . . . if you press it on paper it makes a black mark! Rain Man, well on his way to victory, suddenly becomes distracted by counting the number of hairs on Vic's back. Gump contin-ues to marvel at his discovery thru a series of meaningful doodles on the multiplication table: "I luv Momma" . . . "Foresst rools" . . . etc. Rain Man once again moves toward victory, but a militant faction of Gump fanatics begins to throw boxes of matches on the field to slow his progress. Vic Tayback, in a surprise move, rules that Gump's tables have been filled in, since it was never established that any actual math had to be done. Gump is off in a flash, reaching an almost superhuman speed! Alas, he has run the wrong direction . . . leading to a wonderful heartfelt sequel in which Gump meets many world leaders and famous people in his wonderful heartfelt quest to reach the end of the field from the opposite side. Rain Man, in his meandering manner, finally reaches the end of the field in a few days. Victory! The swell of people rushing in to congratulate Rain Man causes him to begin yelling uncontrollably, at which point Vic Tayback steps in to punch him in the mouth.

—*Rob Souza (Phoenix, Arizona; icewarr@aztec.asu.edu)*

Gump wins easily. See, I'm not voting for the wussy Gump of the movie, but the serious butt-kicking, well-hung, girlfriend screwing, foul-mouthed ex-marine combat vet of the book. Gump jumps up from that table, beats the living $#!+ out of Rain Man, trashes the entire area, lays down covering fire over the judges, and runs off with the prize.

—*G. Nich*

Rain Man has been rocking and droning softly to himself throughout, and this gives Forrest an idea he once used on his grade-school principal. He starts rocking and keening, perfectly mimicking Rain Man, who is perturbed enough to increase his amplitude and volume. A feedback loop develops, and several seconds later Rain Man runs away screaming.

—*Call me Shane*

Rain Man jumps out to an early lead, but within seconds Gump's "charming, homespun philosophy" destroys Rain Man's concentration. He begins rocking back and forth muttering, "Multiplication's not like chocolate. No, not chocolate. No. No. Multiplication. Multiplication is like peppermint. Yes, definitely peppermint. Not chocolate. No. No."

After about forty-five minutes, Gump completes his multiplication table, hands it to Tayback, and flies down the field. Tayback begins to suspect that Gump's answers are wrong when he notices that Gump has written "Momma" in every blank. Tayback is about to disqualify Gump when a Presidential Task Force on Outcome Based Education arrives on the scene.

A representative from the ACLU points out that it would be discrimination to disqualify Gump merely because he is cerebrally differentially-abled and has chosen to expand his horizons beyond the traditional Western concepts of mathematics.

Tayback gives in and declares Gump the winner. Unfortunately, no one told Gump to stop running, so he has now disappeared into the distance, never to be seen again. I love a happy ending.

—*Dr. Dave*

Each competitor attacks the multiplication table in his patented way. Rain Man mumbles out the answers so fast, he appears to be speaking in tongues. Forrest calmly grabs his math-colored Crayola and begins to color all the squares.

This is where the seconds come in. Cruise explains to Raymond that he must write the answers, but Raymond tells his brother that he "can't handle the answers." Cruise begins raising his voice, shouting at his slower brother: "Show me the math! Show me the math!" Raymond complies, just to make his brother stop with the annoying catchphrase. Mel checks Raymond's answers and allows him to proceed to the next stage. Meanwhile, in Gumpy's corner, Momma Field calmly tells Forrest that he can't color the boxes, he must solve the math and write the correct answer. Such complex instructions are received with a patented Gump-stare™. Forrest submits his first attempt, only to have Mel scream: "One times one does not equal chocolate, you dingy! You're worse than Vera." Field tries to curry Mel's favor by offering herself to him and shouting, "You want me! You really, really want me!" To no avail—Mel's heart will always belong to Alice; Forrest must complete the math.

Once away from the table, Rain Man begins wandering all over the field, but nowhere near the finish line. Cruise tries everything to direct Raymond in the right direction. Raymond wants to do some driving but the Porsche is in the shop because it fell into the lake when Lestat went driving wearing only his underwear and sunglasses. In desperation Cruise tries to lure Rain Man to the finish line by telling him there are chocolate-covered shrimp at the finish line. Gump's head snaps up and, in an effort to find the reward, he dashes to the finish line, knocking over everyone on the Field (who was already lying down). Since Forrest left the table without completing the math, Mel has no choice but to disqualify Gump and declare Rain Man the winner by default. Nobody said it was going to be pretty.

—*HotBranch!*

Dennis Rodman vs. RuPaul

THE SETTING

The Date: June 24, 1998

The Location: The Delta Center, Salt Lake City, Utah

The Event: Game 7 of the NBA Finals between the Chicago Bulls and the Utah Jazz. The locker rooms and press booths are teeming with action. Something is amiss, however. Seems that ticket takers are being confronted with two kinds of tickets this evening . . .

As the players take the court for pregame warm-ups, they notice a huge stage at one end of the floor. Curious, Michael

Jordan heads over to see what's up, where he bumps into none other than Whitney Houston. Whitney explains to him that they're setting up for "Up with Chycks," a nationwide tour of music's hottest female pop stars. Michael explains that they're supposed to play the final and most important NBA game of the year.

Suddenly, the crowd starts getting restless. With the arena half filled with crazed Jazz fans and half filled with crazed Chycks fans, people have started figuring out that something has to give. And the twenty thousand or so fans waiting outside aren't too happy either.

But since both parties did schedule the Delta Center for the same night, who should give in? It is quickly decided that a one-on-one fight at center court will decide who gets to stay. Whitney goes to her camp to pick the strongest among them. Michael goes to the two teams, where they decide on sending out their scariest.

The lights are cut, and into the spotlight at center court enter our two combatants. For the Bulls, clad in black leather tights, a white silk blouse, spike heels, and a pink feather boa, stands Dennis Rodman. For the Chycks, decked out in a full sequined evening gown, also with spike pumps, is RuPaul. So, Steve, who wins this nationally televised "cat" fight?

THE COMMENTARY

STEVE: Is there really a contest at all here? Dennis Rodman will win this one in less time than it takes Michael Jordan to sell a Big Mac. Let's just look at the facts. Dennis Rodman is a professional athlete, in tip-top shape. He works out regularly, both on and off the court. On the other hand, RuPaul is hardly what I'd call fit. I'm sorry, but StairMasters, NordicTracks, and Buns of Steel videos are just not going to cut it. Rodman will so overpower RuPaul that (s)he will go crying back to her dressing room and pout. Either that or she'll get turned on.

And, of course, Rodman has experience beating up on defenseless people. Rodman's patented Kick To The Groin™, which he used against that cameraman, will easily apply to the situation here. RuPaul's only defense is his bizarreness. She's simply not used to getting into fights, because most people simply run away in fear at the sight of her. Obviously, Rodman will not fall under this category. He sees this "unique fashion" every morning in the bathroom mirror. And if not there, then possibly in the bed next to him in the form of Madonna. The end result is that the game will be played (on schedule even), and RuPaul goes back to entertaining the yuppies on VH1.

BRIAN: Steve, I am shocked that you would desecrate the Buns of Steel! Do you not comprehend their power? Thanks to the Buns of Steel video series, RuPaul rolls a Honda and plays workout tapes by Fonda, but RuPaul does have a motor in the back of her Honda. That's right, Steve: RuPaul got Back™. And with Back comes endurance, kicking power, and an all around 'tude, each superior to those of the relatively flat-bunned Rodman.

And let's not forget that Rodman cross-dresses merely to get attention and to make himself marketable. Deep down, he's a basketball player first. RuPaul, on the other hand, means it. This is his life! This is what he does! And when put in a pressure situation, their true natures will come out. RuPaul will claw, kick, and scratch, while Rodman will do what he usually does when he gets hit: take a dive to try and draw the technical. As he hits the parquet, he'll look up for the ref who isn't there, and the crowd will cheer RuPaul as the victor!

And even if Rodman keeps pace, consider where this match is being held. Utah. What do they have in Utah? MORMONS!

Clearly, these moral police will not stand for such a display in their capital, so they must intervene. But who shall they send? Why the most famous Mormons, of course: the Osmonds. Wanting to help his sister in music, the Soldier of Love™ blinds Rodman with his purple sequined socks and Dennis goes down. RuPaul ends it with a quickly placed spike to the locale that Rodman has become so famous for targeting.

STEVE: I have to differ with your Osmond analysis. Sure, they will send out Donny to stand up for the righteous, but he will go after RuPaul, not Rodman. After all, RuPaul is *competition* for Marie—helping RuPaul is not going to help Marie in the slightest. Also, lest you forget, they love their sports in Utah. Basketball is big, and they're going to want to watch their game. They won't let anything stand in their way. And not only are sports big, but so is conservatism. I don't think a crowd in Utah is going to be very interested in an Up with Chycks™ rally. Bring on the game!

Just the other night I was watching TV and happened to catch both RuPaul (on VH1) and Rodman (on MTV). Now, it doesn't take a genius to realize that anything on MTV is going to destroy anything on VH1, and this match-up is no exception. Let's compare: VH1 has shows featuring David Cassidy, MTV has shows featuring Jenny McCarthy. Verdict: MTV. VH1 has commercials with Ms. Piggy selling potato chips, MTV has commercials with psycho skateboarders and sky divers who drink Mountain Dew by the gallon. Verdict: MTV. I could go on and on with numerous examples. The point is that MTV rocks, and that anything on it will always be victorious over the thirtysomething-targeted programming on VH1.

Finally, for the record, I would like to point out that after watching RuPaul on TV (I watched for almost an entire minute in the interest of writing this commentary before the pain became unbearable), I have to say that he really is a big sissy. I daresay he would be more of a match for Gilligan or Pee-wee.

BRIAN: Oh, you betray yourself, Steve. Have your ethical standards sunk so low that you will utter ANYTHING in order to justify your deranged points of view? If you claim that VH1 is weakened by showing Miss Piggy commercials, then what of the "powerful Muppet Mystique factor" you speak of in *ALF v. E.T.*? (see p. 104) This powerful mystique is surely enough to overpower anything mustered up by those direction-less, Dew-slammin', angst-spewin', whiny-song-listenin', knee-pad-wearin' idiots that give our generation a bad name. And if you want further proof that VH1 is, in fact, superior to MTV: VH1 shows videos. The last time MTV showed a video, I was in junior high and Duran Duran still rocked.

But let's get back to the subject, shall we? Let's look at how well these two divas are trained for this fight. RuPaul has got some incredible experience from her Up with Chycks™ tour: fighting with the Indigo Girls for dates, boxing out Wynonna for mirror space, bitch-slapping Debbie Gibson on a daily basis just 'cause he can. Who has Rodman gone up against and won? Frank Brickowski? Hardly an impressive résumé, Steve. And all of his battles are waged in high-tops. When it comes to high *heels*, Rodman won't have the experience or the maneuverability that RuPaul will have. Since RuPaul is a full-time drag queen and not a mere sideshow freak, his extralong heels will be second nature, and he will dance circles around the stumbling Rodman.

THE OUTCOME

Dennis Rodman (66%) slam-dunks RuPaul (34%).

THE PEANUT GALLERY™

I read somewhere that to prepare for his role, RuPaul engages in . . . how shall I say this . . . tucking.

This means that Dennis can rev up his foot and try to ring the doorbell with all his might, but there ain't nobody home. There ain't no "pick" to pick and roll. Et cetera.

While Rodman pokes away aimlessly at the gone gonads, RuPaul has an obvious choice of attack point.

Two words: Nipple ring.

—Thinkmaster General

Dennis Rodman nails seven-foot basketball players with his deadly elbows; he kicks, punches, and makes them weep like little girls. RuPaul nails Elton John and makes him giggle like a little girl.

—Baron Samedi

I don't even think there will be a fight. I'll give anyone hundred to one odds that Dennis shows up in a wedding dress, and he and RuPaul get married to promote both his book and her show. After Dennis kicks the priest in the groin after mistaking the Bible he was holding for a camera, the new lovebirds go off to some suitably bizarre place and live a happy existence as man and husband/wife.

—El Squid De La Munchies

Gary Coleman vs. Webster

THE SETTING

It's midnight in Watts, but the evening is just getting started. Junkies throughout Washed-Up Alley, the hangout for out-of-work former child actors, are awaking from their drug-induced comas to begin their nightly rituals. From the darkness appears one of the many once-famous stars looking for a little action. And, upon encountering a broke and strung out Dana Plato, Webster thinks he's found it. He strikes up a conversation with the desperate yet semiconscious Plato, and is just starting to get somewhere when—

"Hey! Back off the lady!" Webster turns to see an enraged Gary Coleman staring him down. "She's an old friend, and she doesn't need you in her face!"

"Well, I know what I don't need," snarls Webster, "is some punk in my face. Looks like someone needs to teach you some manners." Webster reaches into his coat pocket and pulls out a pair of brass knuckles, the weapon of choice in Washed-Up Alley. Coleman does the same, and the two warriors face off.

So, Steve, who do you like in this backstreet battle over the bank-robbing babe?

THE COMMENTARY

STEVE: Brian, there's no question about this one. Gary Coleman in the first round. You have to take into consideration all of the things Gary has going for him.

First, let's not forget where he got his start—on the streets of Harlem. For the first part of his life he LIVED the street fight. He's familiar with the atmosphere, and he knows what it takes to win. He has learned the school of hard knocks from his older brother Willis, and has probably gotten used to taking punches from him too.

Second, just look at them! Gary must have at least fifteen pounds on poor runt-boy Webster. Fifteen pounds of Webster-smashing muscle. Webster's bones are small and fragile, just like toothpicks compared to the might and raw power of Coleman.

Listen, Webster's going to realize within two seconds of entering that ring that his big daddy is not there to protect him this time. Acting cute and innocent won't save him from Gary's wrath. All I can say is that things aren't going to be pretty for runt-boy Webster.

BRIAN: As usual, your simplistic analysis leaves you falling way short of reality. True, maybe Coleman learned a few things on the street, but Webster was raised by Alex Karras, one of the most feared linemen in NFL history. Imagine Webster hanging with Dick Butkus, Bubba Smith, Mean Joe Greene, and several people from those "Less Filling, Tastes Great" commercials when Alex has them over for poker. You think they didn't teach Webster a few tricks of the trade? Webster's gonna have more moves than any street punk Coleman may have met up with.

And, yes, Gary has the size. But if this isn't the epitome of a David and Goliath scenario, I don't know what is. Much like the great Achilles, Coleman has one undeniable weakness: one kidney punch and he's praying for dialysis. With Webster's small size comes quickness. As Coleman's waste-filled blood slows him down, Webster can dodge the first few shots, and move in behind him for the fight-ending lower-back rabbit punches. Webster in thirty seconds on a TKO. Willis himself will throw in the towel to prevent Gary from drowning in a sea of his own blood and urine.

STEVE: Brian, you have nobly defended Webster, but your arguments are as weak as Webster himself. True, there are examples in history of the meek conquering the mighty, but they are few and far between. Much more numerous are instances of the mighty prevailing. Genghis Khan, Alexander the Great, the Soviet Union in Czechoslovakia, and any NFC team crushing the Buffalo Bills. Yes, there are even those who said that the Bills had a chance to win one of their Super Bowls. We have seen that they were fooling themselves. Just as you are.

And do you really think that Karras and Co. bothered to teach Webster all their tricks? First of all, their tricks all rely on great strength and leverage, like how to body-slam some-one, how to give someone a head-slap or leg-whip. Webster is physically incapable of performing such moves. Second, I doubt they would all hang around together as you say. Most likely, as soon as the camera was off, Karras was ordering Webster around, making him shine his shoes or go fetch him a beer. Webster has only learned fear and submission from his onscreen dad.

BRIAN: Examples in history of the meek conquering the mighty are few and far between??!! What kind of revisionist history are you following? Are we forgetting the Revolutionary War, or the British defeat of the Spanish Armada?! What about the Americans beating the mighty Russians to the moon? What about the Miracle on Ice™—Lake Placid, 1980?! Webster's got the same heart, and, dare I say, Eye of the Tiger™, as Rocky, Rocky, Rocky!!

And not only do you not know history, but you know precious little about the battles in the NFL trenches. What makes a player great? Size, speed, and strength make him good, but it's the ability to overpower a man larger and stronger using proper technique that makes a lineman great. The Lite crowd will see Webster's size, and realize these are skills he must have. Gary better watch out when he meets Webster's version of the Bubba Blackout™. Just as Broadway Joe Namath led the underrated, unappreciated, and overachieving New York Jets to a guaranteed victory, the cocky style and free spirit that is Emmanuel Lewis will lead him to crush the underconditioned, unhealthy, and overconfident Gary Coleman.

THE OUTCOME

Gary Coleman (65%) pummels Webster (35%).

THE PEANUT GALLERY™

It's going to take pride to win this fight, which leaves only one competitor standing: Webster. I've seen Gary Coleman on TV making pitches for the Psychic Friends Hotline, for heaven's sake! He can't have a scrap of self-esteem left. While Gary "phones it in," Webster delivers an NFL-caliber clothesline to end it early. Even Dionne Warwick could have predicted this one.

—Call me Shane

As the two miniature pugilists exchange blows, Webster is distracted by an argument between his adoptive TV parents. George Papadapolis is proud that the boy is finally showing some moxie, while Katherine Calder-Young Papadapolis is afraid that their "little treasure" will get hurt. The distraction is nullified when Mrs. Garrett shows up with some cookies for Coleman and Plato. Mrs. Garrett's shriek allows Webster to drop Coleman with a roundhouse kick that he will recall later as sky-high, but that "Dialysis Man" will remember as being right to the family jewels.

While Coleman is writhing on the ground holding his 'nads in agony, Webster will use his size-one shoe to stomp on Coleman's throat, effectively ending the fight.

—HotBranch!

Pee-wee Herman vs. Gilligan

THE SETTING

As the sun begins to dip into the ocean, the clamor coming from a large hut on a remote tropical island continues to grow. From outside, the excitement and tension can be heard and even smelled. Inside is an amazing spectacle. Hundreds of natives are crammed together, raising the temperature even higher than what the hot, equatorial sun brings to this strange place. Wads of a worthless Micronesian currency are quickly changing hands. The loud bantering of the bet takers is quieted as the two warriors enter the ring. On one side, clad in a thong and a headband, stands Gilligan with broken glass glued to the back of his hands. Across from him: Pee-wee

Herman, similarly clad and armed, sweat already glistening on his 105-pound frame. Who wins in this underworld, no-holds-barred, one-on-one kung fu flurry to the death? For extra motivation: If Pee-wee wins, he gets his old bike back (stolen before the match, not by Gilligan); if Gilligan wins, he gets a new shirt.

(NOTE: To beginners, the obvious motivation for Gilligan would be to get off the island. But as history has proven time and time again, whenever getting off the island is at stake, Gilligan screws up, and it wouldn't be a fair fight. Thus the incentive of a doubled wardrobe.)

THE COMMENTARY

STEVE: There is no question here. Pee-wee will be the victor. First of all, remember Pee-wee's association with bikers. He is one of them. He will fight dirty and will do whatever is necessary to win. This is because his bike is his life. Without his bike he is nothing. He traveled across the country facing innumerable obstacles in an effort to locate his prized possession. A mere fight with Gilligan is nothing compared to this.

Pee-wee is no stranger to the evil side of human nature. Deep down, Pee-wee has powerful emotions (including, dare I say, the Rage™) which will provide the fire to win this match. The existence of these powerful emotions can be verified by 1) his arrest for indecent exposure and 2) wearing saddle shoes. Another testament to his evil nature is that satanic laugh. Heh-heh! Yes, I'm afraid Gilligan will be forced to endure another twenty-five years of reruns in his same red shirt.

BRIAN: Oh, to live in that simplistic world you make for yourself, Steve. I've seen a lot of bikers and I'm afraid sailors are ten times tougher. Not only can they cuss better, but you learn to defend yourself when you're forced to wear those silly white hats. Point in fact: The sailor from the Village People kicked the biker's butt on a daily basis (he may have done other things as well, but that's beyond the scope of this discussion).

Besides, Gilligan is a proven leader. After all, it is Gilligan's Island. What does Pee-wee have named after him? A playhouse? Ooooh. Makes me think of that dorky giraffe from Toys "Я" Us. And lest you forget: "If not for the courage of the fearless crew, the Minnow would be lost (the Minnow would be lost)." Is Pee-wee awarded such virtues by his theme song? I thought not.

And if you want the Rage™, look no further than Gilligan. Skipper constantly browbeats him; he was forced by the writers to wear a grass skirt on more than one occasion; he has to make everything out of coconuts; despite constant efforts, he never could hook up with Ginger OR Mary Ann; he hasn't had a decent acting job since. The guy is a walking time bomb. Yes, Pee-wee may want his bike back, but Gilligan, new shirt or not, is going to snap. Following the fight with Pee-wee, he'll go on a five-state killing spree before being shot on an escalator in a suburban JCPenney outside Flint, Michigan.

STEVE: I watch *Gilligan's Island* every weekday morning, and I'm afraid I'm going to have to set you straight on the Ginger/Mary Ann thing. Take the time when the castaways have a fresh fruit/vitamin scare. There is one fresh orange on the island, and it is Gilligan's. Everyone wants it and is trying to butter him up to get it. Ginger struts over and whispers in Gilligan's ear, then plants a hot and steamy kiss squarely on Gilligan's lips. It's clear what she's willing to offer for the orange. Gilligan: "Gosh, I don't think so, Ginger" (or something like that). Gilligan, HELLO! Anybody home? He had his chance, but blew it big.

Oh yeah, the fight. (I get carried away sometimes . . .) So who's teaching Gilligan to fight? Skipper? He's a tub of lard. In fact, I think Gilligan could take Skipper, but that's for another day. Gilligan has no experience and no rage. The only thing that can save Gilligan is a super workout regimen devised by the Professor which will have him benching five hundred pounds within a week. (I think it involves bamboo and coconuts in some weird way). Since there's no time for that, Pee-wee wins within five minutes.

Finally, you have to remember that Gilligan is wearing a red shirt. We've all seen what effect those have on performance. Just watch any old *Star Trek* episode. You're almost guaranteed to see the guy in the red shirt get blown up, zapped, or turned into a small cube and then crushed at least once per episode. The Curse of the Red Shirt™ will flow over to Gilligan, ensuring his loss.

BRIAN: Looks like I'll have to set you straight on this whole Ginger/Mary Ann thing, Steve. The orange incident you're referring to is actually proof of how smart Gilligan is. (For those readers who aren't sure what episode we're talking about, it's the one where they almost get off the island.) Ginger's a tease, everyone knows that. Gilligan's too smart to fall for her siren song. And let's say she was willing to go all the way. That means she's willing to go all the way with anybody, and probably has. Are you suggesting that Gilligan give in to her so that he can get scurvy and VD? No way. It's these kind of street smarts that will get Gilligan the victory.

And while you ask who's going to teach Gilligan to fight, I ask who's going to teach Pee-wee to fight? Or, more relevantly, who's going to teach him to fight with only one hand free? Cap'n Carl?! Pee-wee has no real friends (sure, he's got Mr. Breakfast, but how does that help him?). If he did have any real friends then we all could have avoided that embarrassing movie theater scene. Gilligan has plenty of friends, namely Skipper and the Professor. With Skipper's seaworthy fighting knowledge and the Professor's aforementioned Coconuts of Steel™ workout, Gilligan will be a fighting machine compared to what Pee-wee has to offer. With the knowhow, the strength and the Rage™, not only will Pee-Wee not get his bike back, but he will be beaten to death with it.

THE OUTCOME

Gilligan (56%) shipwrecks Pee-Wee (44%).

THE PEANUT GALLERY™

Did you ever notice that whenever the castaways on *Gilligan's Island* turn on the radio, the announcer is always talking about some story that ends up involving them? Whether it be rock stars, missing robots, or mobsters, they always end up on that small uncharted island. This cannot possibly be a coincidence. Gilligan is clearly the mastermind behind a supersecret organization bent on protecting the free world.

From his remote island base, Gilligan can act in complete secrecy while enjoying the benefits of a warm tropical climate. He is conveniently surrounded by a crack team of unwitting accomplices: the Howells (the money men), the Professor (research and development), Skipper (security), Ginger (espionage/recreation), and Mary Ann (I could tell you, but I'd have to kill you). By "chance," he influences important people and impacts world events without a soul outside that island even knowing he exists. And his fellow castaways never see beyond his clever clumsy facade to see how he again and again foils any chance of escape so he may continue with his anonymous work.

Pee-wee, who is clearly a secret agent sent to corrupt America's youth, has been lured to this island paradise to be liquidated. By the time he realizes the trap, it's too late. A week later, the radio broadcasts that entertainer Pee-wee Herman's dead body was discovered by a fishing boat off the coast of Oahu. Later examination reveals baffling wounds possibly caused by an exploding coconut.

—Paul Golba

The fight begins with both warriors circling each other, trying to spot a weakness in the other's initial position. When the tension is too thick to cut with a Ginsu, Pee-wee makes the fatal mistake of exposing himself, while forgetting that there is broken glass on his hands. As he starts to shout "Made you look!" he quickly realizes that his Pee-wee wee-wee has been severed and is lying on the floor of the hut.

This is the opening that Gilligan has been waiting for. As Pee-wee frantically tries to tape his privates back on, Gilligan launches himself in Pee-wee's direction with arms and legs flailing. Whether Gilligan actually connects with any of his blows will forever be a mystery, because Pee-wee is an immobile heap on the ground, bleeding to death from a self-inflicted pecker wound.

—HotBranch!

Flipper vs. Jaws

THE SETTING

In a battle for ocean supremacy, Flipper and Jaws prepare to duel to the death. The arena is a parcel of tropical ocean waters (about a square mile) from which all other sea creatures have been painstakingly removed to avoid distractions or outside assistance. Both contestants are highly motivated. Jaws is hungry. He hasn't eaten for days, and the chum in the water isn't helping. Flipper has been hypnotized by a leading dolphin hypnotist with a one-word phrase: "kill." The two are simultaneously released in close proximity. Only one will survive.

THE COMMENTARY

BRIAN: Is it just me or is this a complete no-brainer? Flipper in a rout, Steve. Yes, Flipper has been subconsciously programmed to kill, but remember he's still the smartest dolphin who has ever lived (and, if those people from Earth Day™ are correct, dolphins are the smartest animals on the planet). With cunning forethought and strategic military planning reminiscent of Patton, Flipper will lure Jaws closer and closer, both going at tremendously high speeds, descending toward the ocean floor. (I know Flipper's an air breather, but if anyone can do it, Flipper can.) Then, just as the two are reaching interstate-type velocities and are only a few feet away from the coral rocks below, Flipper unveils his greatest weapon: turning radius. Picture a Porsche making a hairpin turn at fifty mph followed by an eighteen-wheeler doing the same. Jaws jack-knifes into the coral reef and will be only slightly less disfigured than when he smiled with that air canister in his mouth.

STEVE: Have you been smoking kelp again? Jaws is going to eat Flipper alive. Maybe you need a little refresher from *Jaws*. Jaws is one tough cookie. Your little scenario makes me (and him) laugh. Coral actually hurting Jaws? He was harpooned multiple times, shot several times, hungry, and tired from dragging barrels around all night, and yet this didn't stop him. After this lengthy ordeal, he was still strong enough to drag a fishing boat backwards and nearly pull the transom from the boat. Flipper hasn't seen this kind of might before, and he won't ever again, since this will be his last stand.

We know from the movies that there are only a limited number of ways to kill Jaws. The first is by exploding a compressed air tank in his mouth. The second is by getting him to bite a high-voltage wire. Since neither of these seem to be around, and Flipper is incapable of using either, then Jaws is inde-structible. It's only a matter of time.

BRIAN: Correction, Steve: What we learn from the movies is that even if Flipper had an air tank or a high-voltage wire it wouldn't do him any good. Because whenever Jaws shows up, he *has* to die, and he has to do so in a *new* way each time. By simply appearing in this match Jaws has sealed his fate. And since several of the obvious methods have been used, and since Flipper lacks opposable thumbs, you can guarantee Flipper will use his speed ("Flipper, Flipper, faster than light-ning") and cunning to slice Jaws up on that *razor-sharp* coral easier than a hot Ginsu through a tin can. Looks like you need your own little refresher on coral topography, Steve.

And, besides, what skills does Jaws really have? Sure, he may be good at picking off little kids in the coastal villages of Connecticut, but who wouldn't be? I could do that. But Flipper can do tricks, he can communicate, and he can always catch the bad guy. "What's that, Flipper? The smugglers are getting away and little Timmy O'Toole's boat is sinking? You call the Coast Guard and I'll get Porter." He's like a wet Lassie! And since Jaws is clearly a bad guy, his minutes are numbered. Once Flipper dispatches Jaws with his patented Dorsal Shiver™, he'll skim off to Alaska to save Free Willy from an oil slick, much to the chagrin of moviegoers everywhere.

STEVE: Correction, Brian: This isn't a movie, it's a Grudge Match™, and therefore Jaws does *not* have to die. In fact, he will likely come out of this unscathed. Also, I'm not sure which is funnier, your little coral-smashing scheme or how you actu-ally believe it will work. And I fail to see how any of Flipper's tricks are going to help him. By your reasoning, David Copperfield, who can also do tricks and communicate, is also capable of defeating Jaws. Sure, maybe he could make Jaws disappear temporarily amidst a light and music show, but Jaws would suddenly reappear and gulp him down in one bite.

A final important factor to consider is what is said in the original *Jaws*. All Jaws does is eat, swim, and make baby sharks. That's only three things. When you only do three things, by golly, you do them well. Flipper, with all his "tricks," is spread too thin, and will quickly fall to a creature who does nothing but eat helpless sea creatures like Flipper. Jaws is a pro, doing his thing, like Tiger Woods getting a birdie, Seattle Slew winning a race, Babe Ruth hitting a home run, or Latrell Sprewell choking a coach. And when a pro is at his best, he's unbeatable.

THE OUTCOME

Flipper (53%) makes bait out of Jaws (47%).

THE PEANUT GALLERY™

Bad news for your strategy, Brian. Coral is technically a living thing, and so will be among the sea creatures removed from the arena. Flipper will discover this, emit a few squeaks that, if properly translated, would get his show at least a TV-14, and then die messily.

—*Call me Shane*

Jaws is a shark, which is a type of fish. A good example of a fish would be my pet goldfish, Beck. After Beck is fed, he tends to repeatedly ram his head into the ceramic castle in his aquarium. This pointless and self-destructive behavior puts him miles ahead of mammalian creatures such as dolphins, or their surface counterparts, my cubicle-dwelling coworkers.

I prefer the fish method of self-flagellation; at least it's more direct. Jaws in thirty minutes—he'll try to ram the coral reef into submission, and then get hungry. Flipper will just try to network.

—Thinkmaster General

Flipper has a nice set of teeth, designed to chew small fish and pose for toothpaste ads. Shark teeth have a single purpose: to rip stuff to shreds. When Flipper tells Jaws, "reeeep reeeeeeeeepppp rep reeeep" (Dolphin for "My, what big teeth you have"), Jaws won't bother with formalities, like the wolf in "Little Red Riding Hood."

Flipper is cute, that's true, but cute won't cut it in the squared circle of water. The formerly crystal blue water will now be an ominous shade of purple, tainted by the blood of a dolphin pretender (how did Dan Marino get into this discussion?). Unlikely, you say? I offer you George Foreman as proof that the fat, old, lazy, and cheeseburger-laden CAN be world champions. Jaws is the George Foreman of the sea, and Flipper is the chicken of the sea. Sorry, Charlie . . .

—HotBranch!

The Bandit vs. CHiPs

THE SETTING

Eastbound and down, loaded up and trucking, we're gonna do what they say can't be done. . . . On a hot summer afternoon, Ponch and Jon see a black blur speeding through the west side of Los Angeles. It's the Bandit! He's transporting a carful of illegal tuna-safe dolphin from the beach to Las Vegas. He's got to make it there in two hours or the deal with Boss Hogg is off! Ponch and Jon must catch him before he reaches the state line. (They, unlike Buford T. Justice, realize they have no power outside of their jurisdiction.) Both parties have CBs and can call for backup or help from other vehicles. Does justice prevail, or does the bad guy drive off into the sunset with Sally Field?

THE COMMENTARY

STEVE: This match-up is certainly a tough one! Ponch and Jon are California's finest, and always seem to get their man in the end. Bandit, on the other hand, always seems to find the way out somehow (just like Captain Kirk). However, I'm going to have to go with Bandit. Since the *CHiPs* boys are working under a time constraint, there will be inevitable problems. They always require at least an hour to catch the bad guy, a luxury they might not have in this scenario. Also, it'll be very easy for ol' Burt to detain Ponch and Jon. All he has to do is swerve wildly on the freeway. Cars behind him will lose control and form a huge heaping pile of wreckage and carnage. Of course, Ponch and Jon will have to stop and rescue the trapped motorists. Then, just as they free the motorists, the whole pile goes up in a huge fireball. By this time, Burt is miles away, heading to Vegas with his payload, and he will still have time to stop off at an All-You-Can-Eat wedding chapel and get married to Sally.

BRIAN: I can't believe you fell for one of the oldest plots in television, Steve! Of course Bandit is going to cause a lot of trouble in L.A. (Although I doubt it will be as severe and sadistic as you suggest. Bandit is actually a very deep and caring guy.) And, of course, the *CHiPs* boys will have to stop and help. But that's early in the show. Was there ever a *CHiPs* episode where the bad guy didn't just barely get away from Ponch and Jon in the first twenty minutes? NO! Ponch and Jon have to have their own lives and the lives of others risked before their capturing of the Bandit in the end is theatrically complete. They have to get the rage/personal vendetta, otherwise there's no program! From watching *CHiPS* and *Smokey and the Bandit I-VII*, we know this has to come down to the wire, somewhere very, very close to the California/Nevada border.

Bandit will get a lead in L.A., but then he'll get cocky. Stop off at a truck stop. Get some lunch. Ponch and Jon will catch up. And when they do, and since we are in the *CHiPs* universe, all they have to do is get the Bandit to run off the road for a second. For wherever he does run off the road, there's going to be an abandoned green 1977 Pinto just waiting. BOOM!! The End™.

Out in the desert, there are no washed-out bridges to jump. Out in the desert, there is nowhere to hide. Out in the desert, no one can hear you scream.

STEVE: Brian, maybe you can hear me scream this: WRONG! You're forgetting that the bad guys who Paunch and Jon catch are always repeat offenders. They hang around the area and commit the same crime over and over. Of course they're going to get caught! Even the "Half" from *Cop and a Half* could catch them. Once the *CHiPs* boys stop, they're never going to catch Bandit, as he'll be flying along at a hundred miles per hour through the desert. And if, by some chance, they did manage to catch up to him, he'd be on the CB to his truckin' buddies:

Bandit: Breaker one-nine, this is Bandit, I got a few smokeys on my tail.
Trucker: No problem, Bandit. You can sit in the rockin' chair until the Nevada line.
Bandit: Ten-four, good buddy!

Bandit then rides in complete safety until the Nevada state line. Watch that Bandit run!

And if by some quirk of fate Ponch and Jon do manage to

catch up to the Bandit near the border, then they will still fail in their task. All of a sudden, with the end of the show being near, they will spontaneously freeze-frame in midlaughter. As the credits roll by, the Bandit will look on in bewilderment. Not being susceptible to these annoyingly repetitive pauses, he will easily drive on to victory.

BRIAN: First of all, Steve, you owe an apology to Ponch, to Jon, to Worf, to Harry Callahan, to Mike Stone, and to cops throughout that state for comparing the "Half" from *Cop and a Half* to true California law enforcement officers! Can "Half" run down speeding white Broncos? Does "Half" have the follow-through on his billy-club swing? I don't think so!

Second, sure the criminals in most of the old *CHiPs* shows were morons just asking to be caught. But who's the only guy that ever chased the Bandit? Buford T. Justice??!! Not exactly Wyatt Earp there! Don't even get me started on his nephew. Neither Ponch and Jon nor the Bandit have been pushed to the limit—yet. In the deserts of southern California, the limits will be tested, and somebody will buckle. I say it's the undisciplined and comparatively soft Bandit.

And third, you show your ignorance of this situation by your assertion that the freeze-frame credits would affect Ponch and Jon during the chase. Everyone knows that happens after the major plot points have been resolved and during some whimsical misadventure in the epilogue. Thus, while the Bandit is being hauled away in handcuffs, Ponch's classic smile is frozen several times when Jon sits on a cactus.

THE OUTCOME

The Bandit (61%) escapes CHiPs (39%).

THE PEANUT GALLERY™

Bandit will meet his contact, Takleberry, at the Blue Oyster Bar. Tak will slip Bandit a piece of paper explaining where the canned dolphin can be found. Bandit slips out of the bar, not quite unnoticed. Having raised his eyes from his drink just in time, Ponch realizes that something fishy is going on. After rousing Jon from a tequila coma, California's two finest highway patrolmen head out without any authorization from their superiors.

Just outside the La Brea tarpits, Ponch and Jon spot Bandit's vehicle and the game is afoot! Naturally, it's rush hour and the freeways are blocked tighter than a frog's behind in water, but that matters not one bit, since Bandit is getting traffic guidance (and lecherous looks) from the Flying Nun. Ponch and Jon easily maneuver through the traffic despite being on Harleys that are wider than most Honda Civics. The chase moves from the freeway to the L.A. sewer system, where two cyborgs are chasing each other in a fight for possession of a snot-nosed brat. In a geographically impossible cut, the scene suddenly changes to Lombard Street in San Francisco: Ponch and Jon look like parallel slalom skiers while Bandit barrels through all the barricades and flower gardens.

Almost two hours have gone by and CHiPs are running out of time: the Nevada border is just over the horizon and Bandit looks to be making a clean getaway. All is not lost. A freak happenstance of nature has made the sun set in the east on this night and Ponch reveals his teeth with a winning smile. The reflection of the sun off Ponch's teeth is aimed at Bandit's gas tank. Bandit is unaware of the impending danger and dies in a gruesome fireball mere yards from the Nevada border. It should be noted that the only surviving item in the vehicle was Burt's rug.

—HotBranch!

Ponch is struck with inspiration. He makes the call to some of his hermanos in East L.A., giving them Bandit's license and his twenty (location, for those of you sane enough not to know CB jargon). Surely they'll help one of their own catch some trailer trash Georgia Anglo.

Wrong! Bandit's working-class, antiauthority appeal strikes a chord in the heart of the barrio. His Trans Am flashes through their neighborhood to cheers, and a roadblock of rusty cars and vendor's carts springs up behind him. Ponch takes his usual spill, landing boots-up in a Dumpster.

—*Call me Shane*

[One] possibility is the Bandit turns into a wimp and tries using Steve's Rockin' Chair. However, this will merely lead to a humiliating defeat. Paunch and Jon will have called up their buddy Worf after losing the Bandit in Los Angeles. Along with Worf will be the rest of the DS9 crew (whenever people from DS9 travel to Earth they always end up going back in time). Therefore the truck that the Bandit escapes into will be none other than the shapeshifting Constable Odo, securing an easy win for the California Highway Patrol. Some might argue that the Federation wouldn't interfere, but remember, the Bandit is hauling dolphins and *Star Trek IV* demonstrated that you are allowed to interfere with the time line if it helps marine mammals.

—*Brendan W. Guy*

Rush Limbaugh vs. Howard Stern

THE SETTING

The Scene: A brisk but sunny morning at Lakehurst, New Jersey, just south of New York City. A small crowd and several TV cameras have gathered around our two competitors, who are already at work preparing for their long flights.

The Competition: Rush Limbaugh and Howard Stern are busy inflating their hot-air balloons, while their crews load provisions into the baskets. However, no propane tanks are present. These balloons are powered by their occupant's self-generated hot air. Each must propel his balloon by this method only, in an endurance race of epic proportions.

The Course: As there is such a surplus of hot air present in this competition, the race will be around the world. Checkpoints will be set up in Paris, Moscow, Tokyo, Honolulu, San Francisco, and Chicago. The finish line is back at Lakehurst. The contestants may stop as needed for food and water (Rush insisted on this). First one across the finish line (with balloon) wins. The referee of this match is Morton Downey, Jr., who was ineligible to compete due to his show sucking so bad. His decisions are final.

THE COMMENTARY

BRIAN: I see this race very close at San Francisco, with Limbaugh having a slight edge as they sail over the Golden Gate Bridge. Limbaugh's surplus of hot air resulting from a Democrat living in the White House™ will ensure this lead. But the same thing that gives him all that air, his tremendous girth, will also be his downfall. It all boils down to two simple letters: mv (that's momentum, for those of you in Rio Linda™). On each leg of the race, Rush gets a slow start due to that whole "a body at rest" thing. But once he reaches top speed, he blows past Stern, laughing all the way with his cigar firmly clutched in his formerly nicotine-stained fingers. But upon approaching each checkpoint, Limbaugh must slow down more than five hundred miles beforehand so he does not over-shoot it.

And there's the catch! San Francisco and Chicago are too close! If Limbaugh stays at top speed for more than five seconds he'll zip right over Chicago and splash down in Lake Ontario. This is where Stern gets his lead, just chug-chug-chugging along. Of course, Stern gets a bit cocky after Chicago: He laughs and pokes fun at Limbaugh behind him, insults some minorities over Cleveland, apologizes to their relatives as he passes over New Jersey, and lets Limbaugh get close. It's not enough, though, as he wins by 10.4 seconds. Limbaugh hits NYC at full speed in a last-ditch attempt, slams on the brakes immediately, and lands safely in the Azores.

STEVE: Oh, poor, naive Brian. Sometimes I feel sorry for you and your innocent ways. You're forgetting about several factors here. First, there's air resistance. Rush's spherically shaped body and slick hair will give him almost no drag. However, Howard has that huge head of hair and sunglasses, which will slow his progress drastically. Second, as you mentioned, there are the cigars. A few more drops in the bucket of heat generation. Not to mention that the nicotine will cause him to talk at unprecedented speeds, generating enormous amounts of hot air. Third, there is ego. Rush could probably get away without using a balloon at all—his ego will lift him up high. And finally, Rush has his "condom update" song "Up, Up and Away in My Beautiful Balloon" ready to play at a moment's notice. Now that's awesome power.

As you can see, really this is no contest at all. Howard will make a valiant attempt, but will start to lose ground over the Atlantic. Also, as he travels over Europe and Asia, no one will understand English, and with no one appreciating him, Howard will become disheartened and lose major ground. By the time he gets to Hawaii and his listenership is back, it is too late. Rush is already crossing the Delaware and is descending over Jersey.

Oh no! Rush is so confident of his win that he starts telling the world how great he his. Excess hot air is being produced! The pressure in his balloon is critically high! BOOM! Rush plummets to the ground, but luckily his fall is broken by Morton Downey. Rush is across the finish line, and the remnant of his balloon drifts across the finish line as well. The checkered flag for Rush!

BRIAN: And you call ME the naive one. First of all, in case you haven't noticed, Steve, Rush is huge!!!! He's got more drag than New Orleans on a Saturday night! Stern's as thin as a rail and will slice through the air (to combat the hair problem, he'll just put his quaff up in a bun and buy one of those teardrop-breaking-away Quicksilver helmet things). Second, Stern's got an even bigger ego than Limbaugh! Stern hits on *Baywatch* Babes and thinks he's getting somewhere!! And has Rush ever had a hit movie? Is Rush only on E!? No! Third, if Limbaugh plays more than four notes of that "Up, Up and Away" crap, he'll get dive-bombed by hordes of seagulls even more disgusted at this 70s-revival thing than the rest of the world. Fourth, being over countries where they don't speak English will only serve to boost Stern's spirits. He'll be able to insult millions of people who don't look like him without apology since no one will understand what he's saying in the first place!

And another major factor here is the hot air itself. The rules do not restrict where the hot air comes from, as long as it is self-generated. Well, with the proper diet and an acetylene torch, Fartman will be laying his sonic wake on the Himalayas before Rush has even had a chance to finish his opening dialogue on Whitewater™. True, Rush may have a significant flatulence factor of his own, but he's just not in Fartman's class.

(By the way, Morton Downey, Jr., is unable to make the call after being rushed to the hospital to get his foot surgically removed from his mouth. Again. So his close friend, Richard Bey, comes in to declare Howard the winner.)

STEVE: Brian, sometimes you say things that really scare me and make me think that you should be locked away. I'm a bit confused by your E! comment. Are you trying to say that being on E! exclusively is somehow an advantage? I can't see how being in the company of Downtown Julie Brown and Joan Rivers is going to help Howard Stern complete the race any faster. Unless he's trying to get away from them as fast as possible. But maybe that's just me.

Howard also gets distracted very easily and will have difficulty even finishing the race. Every woman he passes over will cause him to pause while he grabs a megaphone and a pair of binoculars, and tries to talk her into taking off her shirt. He'll also have to pause and plug his book and movie, *Private Parts*, to every person he sees. This is going to cost him valuable time. These distractions will cause him to lose sight of the bigger picture of the balloon race, leading to his imminent defeat.

Finally, a simple name analysis will show that Rush must win. If one looks up Rush in the dictionary, you find words like *rapidity, haste, eagerness,* and *force*. These are obviously words describing someone bound to be victorious in any sort of race. However, the definition of Stern is *pointing backwards,* or *the rear end of a vessel*. Thus, if anything, Howard is going to travel backwards. And anyone who shares part of their name with a chain of restaurant-motels with bright orange roofs doesn't deserve to win.

THE OUTCOME

Howard Stern (52%) out-talks Rush Limbaugh (48%).

THE PEANUT GALLERY™

Rush Limbaugh annoys American politicians. Now consider the media exposure Rush is receiving from this event. The last time Rush stepped on toes, Clinton tried to censor him. Before he knows it, he will be surrounded by Democratic spin doctors in balloons. Not to be outdone, the Republicans send up their contingent, followed by the Media, ACLU, NAACP, Christian Coalition, Operation Rescue, Planned Parenthood, NOW, Lyndon LaRouche, Ross Perot, and some guy in a clown wig carrying a "John 3:16" sign. This fiasco leads to the prompt creation of the Congressional Hot Air and Ballooning Committee, which goes up to investigate. Simply put, Rush is not going anywhere.

—Paul Golba

LAKEHURST (NEW YORK CITY): before liftoff stern will make an appointment at one of the finest hair salons in manhattan. as he reaches the altitude of the jet stream (west to east flow), he will open his hair like a japanese fan and sail across the atlantic with amazing speed.

PARIS: unfortunately, although warned to be on his best behavior, stern will let slip that france is a third world country. while true, this will infuriate the french, who will down stern's balloon with a couple of heavily-armed mirage fighters. fortunately, stern will survive, as he is too thin of a target to show up on radar. rush will catch up and use his conservative rhetoric to pose as charles de gaulle's nephew. the french, overcome by their love of the man who masterminded the maginot line and was overrun by the nazis, will send him on ahead.

MOSCOW: rush will stop for food at the moscow mcdonald's. this will give stern the weeks he needs to apologize profusely and repair his balloon (with the help of the highly technically minded french). while i don't want to minimize rush's ability to gorge himself, there just isn't that much food in russia. therefore, rush will still have a moderate lead when he leaves for tokyo.

TOKYO: stern has closed the gap, using his hair-sail advantage over the siberian wasteland. unfortunately, his rodan-like hairstyle alerts the japanese military as he approaches tokyo. hypersensitive to monster attacks, the japanese down him with surface-to-air missiles. he will survive (see PARIS), but will again need to repair his balloon. fortunately, what took weeks in france takes mere hours in japan. still, rush will have long left the country, being infuriated with the small food portions, high prices, and public transportation.

HONOLULU: rush will make a brief stop for food. oahu is a small island and the food reserves will be depleted quickly. i have to give the u.s. military enough credit to identify that stern is a balloonist and not a russian backfire bomber. rush will lead, but stern will trail closely.

SAN FRANCISCO: after the grueling pacific legs, i see rush with a slight lead. assuming that the bay area liberals do not kill rush and use him as a float for a parade of some sort, rush will make a quick exit, sensing his life is in danger. stern will invariably stop to be the grand marshal of a gay pride parade.

CHICAGO: as the rail link to the bread basket of america, chicago offers rush a chance to truly fill up. he will have access to more rice, wheat, corn, and other complex carbohydrates than anywhere else in the world. this is the first chance rush has had to get a decent meal over the entire trip, and he will make use of it.

FINISH: it's tough to call, but i have to give the edge to rush. i think that rush will overtax even the food transportation network of the chicago area and have to leave for new york to avoid starvation.

—jeff

Mr. T vs. Mr. Clean

THE SETTING

It's summer in a bad section of New Orleans, and the steamy heat is shortening everyone's temper in this seedy, dank, smoke-filled bar, including those of our two contestants. Seated side by side at the bar are Mr. T and Mr. Clean, both of whom have been drinking steadily for several hours. Although they are aware of each other's presence, they have been ignoring each other and drowning their own personal anguishes in whiskey. Mr. T is (still) upset about the cancellation of *The A-Team* as well as losing to Rocky. Mr. Clean just got word that he will lose his job because those damn Scrubbing Bubbles will work for less money. Tempers are running short—neither contestant has anything left to lose.

While reaching for his next drink, Mr. T accidentally spills it all over Mr. Clean. Mr. Clean jumps to his feet in anger! Mr. T, who is already primed for a fight, jumps to his feet as well. The Rage™ glints in both of their eyes—it is clear that only one will walk out of the bar in one piece. Brian, who do you like in this traditional barroom brawl?

THE COMMENTARY

BRIAN: Well, the way I see it, The Rage™ is about a wash. Mr. T's mad about two things (losing *The A-Team*, losing to Rocky); Mr. Clean's mad about two things (losing out to Scrubbing Bubbles, getting drink spilled on him); there's an additional component involving scalp razor burn, but that's a push as well. Despite what my Uncle Olaf always used to say ("Never bet on the white guy"), I gotta go with Mr. Clean. True, all we ever see of the Clean Man is his silly smile in recently polished bathroom tile, but I saw him in one of those bare-fisted contests last week and he beat the crap out of that guy that guarded the plane in *Raiders of the Lost Ark*. He might clean grout as good as Alice, but he's got a rock-solid build on him and a left that Clubber Lang wouldn't see coming.

Besides, just look at the jewelry. Mr. T has got a good seventy-five pounds weighing him down when he's out on the town like this. He's about to OG. But all Mr. Clean has is a relatively light yet daringly bold single hoop earring. (Which, by the way, he's had since high school. That's how he learned to fight.) Moe, the bartender, calls a TKO after ninety seconds (at which point he is overheard saying "What'z da mattah, Mistah T?")

STEVE: You can take your chance on Mr. Clean, but I pity the poor fool who don't pick Mr. T. Mr. Clean is soft from his many years of leeching off innocent homemakers. Others do all the work, and he always jumps in at the last minute and takes all the credit. Kind of like Clinton.

Mr. T is an experienced fighter. He was once the heavyweight champ, after all. He also had a lot of experience bashing in heads with his *A-Team* cronies. He's got the Eye of the Tiger™ back—he's certainly learned his lesson from *Rocky III*. He's ready for the comeback trail, and the first step is conveniently close—Mr. Clean.

I recently had the privilege of skimming through Mr. T's autobiography, and there is a lot to learn about this great man. First, T used to be a bouncer in a bar (big surprise there, eh?). Therefore, if anyone knows how to handle himself in a barroom brawl, it is Mr. T. Second, he also used to be a security guard at concerts. If you can keep drug-crazed moshing street punks off a stage, you can easily handle someone as benign as Mr. Clean.

BRIAN: First of all, for using the overly obvious "I pity the fool" reference in the first sentence of your rebuttal, you receive a ten-minute mute penalty.

Second, how can you just ignore the fact that Mr. T will be weighed down and sluggish from wearing excessive gold? In the scenario we see that Mr. T "jumps to his feet." Well, if you've ever worn a chain, you know it bounces when you jump. Once Mr. T lands, all that gold around his neck will come jerking down, sending several of his upper vertebrae through the barroom floor. Not a pretty sight.

Third, if Mr. Clean never does any work, how did he get so big? Perhaps his "Wax On, Wax Off" regimen is more effective than you give it credit for. And staying one step ahead of grease and grime takes more than just muscle, but cunning as well. It is this kind of cunning that will win the fight for Mr. Clean. As Mr. T moves toward him, Mr. Clean points to the freshly Cleaned™ bar: "Is it wet or is it dry?" As the dim-witted

Mr. T ponders this sanitation enigma, Mr. Clean beats him upside the head with his own two-foot-high Africa-shaped gold medallion.

Fourth, I can't believe I'm arguing with a guy who actually owns Mr. T's autobiography. Where do I find these people?

STEVE: Sure, Mr. T is weighted down with gold, but that is an asset, not a liability. Years of toting that gold around have made him enormously strong. His neck and shoulders are so pumped that he could take upper-body punches all day from someone as weak as Mr. Clean.

So you allege that housework has made Mr. Clean so buff? I don't recall ever seeing any housewives that pumped up from only mopping floors and cleaning countertops. The only possible explanation is that Mr. Clean is on steroids. And we all know from *Rocky IV* that once you get the steroid-laden fighter bleeding, it's all over. Not only will he lose his strength, but once the blood hits the floor, he'll be distracted. He'll have to stop every passerby (he is a salesman, after all) by trying to show off the cleaning abilities of his cleanser on bloodstains. T in one minute.

THE OUTCOME

Mr. T (52%) mops up Mr. Clean (48%).

THE PEANUT GALLERY™

You said this was a traditional barroom brawl . . . doesn't that mean that everyone present has to get involved? So let's analyze who would come in on each side. Mr. Clean is worshipped by hordes of bored homemakers who are so lonely and desperate for human involvement that they are expected (by clever advertisers) to concoct some sort of relationship with a chrome-domed guy on their ammonia bottle. Now, either these housekeepers probably don't hang out in bars or (the possibility I personally feel to be more likely) they may not really even exist. On the other hand, Mr. T was known and loved by crowds of adolescents (remember, he even had a Saturday morning cartoon show), lots of middle-class people living in Nielsen homes, and the usual admiring throngs of emotionally deprived fan-boys. I suspect that a few of these types may be in the bar (unless *The A-Team* reruns are on at this time of the evening) and would come to the aid of their hero. Face it, before Mr. Clean can even yell for mommy, Mr. T and all his fans will be all over the poor guy. Time to mop up with Mr. Clean. . . .

—*JM Massi, Ph.D.*

With two so evenly matched contestants, we have to look at who will be the backup in the barroom brawl. Mr. T will have brought his relatives Ice-T, T-Bone Burnett, T-Bone Walker, and a generation of kids raised on T ball.

Who does Mr. Clean have? Maybe his second cousin Don McLean, and he's due for a beating anyways.

The big plus of the night is that the members of the band Mr. Mister, who aren't able to choose sides, get the tar beaten out of them by all combatants.

—*Thinkmaster General*

Clean runs past Mr. T, who grabs at Clean's earring and pulls it clean off, causing Clean's earlobe to tear.

Clean stands up, touching his hand to his bleeding ear. Mr. Clean is horrified to realize that his blood is staining the floor, and he drops to his knees and starts scrubbing at the mess he has caused. That is the fight-ending mistake. T, wanting desperately to win a fight, starts kicking at Mr. Clean in brutal LAPD fashion.

—HotBranch!

The Prayers: As we all know, T is deeply religious—he must be wearing at least three or four emblems from every major religion. Thus T has the moral advantage.

The Vitamins: T's buffness comes straight from his formative years in those tough-man competitions back when athletes weren't afraid to explore every possible chemical advantage. Just as the televised competitions live on the Deuce, so must the substances live on in T's body.

—Dave C.

Mr. Clean, in a furious series of brutal attacks, strikes Mr. T in every conceivable location but only manages to polish the gold to a brilliant shine. Finally, in an act of utter desperation, Mr. Clean follows up with a blow to the head and turns the mohawk bleach blond, just like Dennis Rodman.

Mr. T is pissed. Instantly, Mr. Clean is in a vise-grip headlock. Suddenly, Mr. T realizes his enemy's weakness—his body is a plastic bottle, just like his product. After a few easy turns, the head comes right off. Mr. T then turns Mr. Clean upside down, pours his innards on the floor and throws the remainder in the recycling bin.

—Paul Golba

Ed. note: Okay, so they're not *exactly* chihuahuas—
but how could we resist this pic?

A Rottweiler vs.
A Rottweiler's Weight in
Chihuahuas

THE SETTING

The Grudge Match investigative crew saunters into a seedy restaurant establishment a few miles south of Tijuana, Mexico. Our ace reporter gives the password and 500,000 pesos (about $6.50) to the bartender and they are escorted to the back. The bartender nods to what appears to be a mirror and the wall buzzes. Through a hidden door (covered by a velvet painting of a matador), our men walk into the back room. There, surrounded by scores of screaming local peasants and Asian businessmen, is a sand-filled pit. At one end is chained a large male Rottweiler, mad as can be. At the other end, all in a small cage, is the Rottweiler's weight equivalent in Chihuahuas. The Chihuahuas are covered in A-1 Sauce (which they hate but the Rottweiler loves) while the Rottweiler is covered in, of course, taco sauce. All of the animals have been kept in extremely small cages over the past thirty days and during that time they have been thumped on the forehead with a wooden spoon at five-minute intervals. Basically, they're all really pissed. They've also all been starved for the past thirty-six hours, so they are extremely hungry but not weak. If the Rottweiler kills all the Chihuahuas and lives, he wins. If he dies and one Chihuahua is left alive, they win. Who do you place your pesos on, Steve, in this Canine Catastrophe South of the Border?

THE COMMENTARY

STEVE: I've given this some careful consideration, and I have to go with the Chihuahuas on this one. Obviously, the Rottweiler will be able to maul each Chihuahua with one bite. However, the Chihuahuas will simply overwhelm the Rottweiler by sheer numbers. Estimating a 120-pound Rottweiler and five-pound Chihuahuas, that gives twenty-four sets of yap-dog teeth. Too much for even a BBQ-sauce-crazed beast to handle. Wow! All those years of engineering calculus certainly paid off for me this time.

One thing you have to remember about Chihuahuas (and all yap-dogs for that matter) is that they are mean. They are pissed at life in general for being so small, and need a destructive outlet for their pent-up rage. A good example of this is the only famous Chihuahua I can think of, Ren from *Ren & Stimpy*. He is evil and mean, with his temper flaring up regularly at the kind-hearted Stimpy. Now imagine twenty-four of these critters, thinking only of tacos. I liken this to frenzied piranhas attacking a helpless foe. Sure, some of them will die.

But in the end, the Rottweiler will fall. I place 22.5 million pesos and a bottle of tequila on the Chihuahuas.

BRIAN: What?!! True, the Chihuahuas have numbers and home court advantage, but those won't be nearly enough. Those little rug rats won't even be able to break the skin on that big dog! That Rottweiler is one hundred plus pounds of yap-dog smashing muscle! Have you ever seen a REAL Chihuahua, Steve? What are they good for? All they ever do is shake and pee on themselves. I don't care how crazed they are; they could even be Old Yeller Rabid Crazy™ and they'd still be shaking in fear too much to take on a kibble or a bit, never mind a Rottweiler. This is like saying twenty-four flies are a match for a bullfrog. No way. No matter how many there are, they can't do any damage to that canine beast.

For just a moment I will give you the benefit of the doubt. Let's say the Chihuahuas are so crazed by the thirty days of confinement/torture that they are actually worth something. At the start of the match, the Rottweiler mauls five of them. The sixth one breaks through and clamps down on the beast's back. While not breaking the skin, he does manage to taste the taco sauce, at which point he says, "This taco sauce is terrible" (and then gets mauled). Another Chihuahua picks up the taco sauce bottle and says, "Hey! This stuff is made in New York City!" (and then gets mauled). All the other Chihuahuas yell "New York City?" and proceed to attack the pit boss. The Rottweiler wins by default as the seventeen remaining Chihuahuas yip out of the ring.

I'm putting 250 million pesos and a six-pack of Corona on the BIG DAWG!!

STEVE: Unfortunately, I have seen Chihuahuas up close, and I can enlighten you on two factors. First, I agree that their teeth have no flesh-tearing power, but their teeth are in fact a mouthful of sharp needles. They are certainly capable of breaking the skin and causing puncture wounds. A little-known fact is that after being bitten repeatedly by a Chihuahua, Dr. Julio Hernandez was inspired to build the world's first—you guessed it—hypodermic needle. Unfortunately, shortly after building his creation, he died from rabies obtained from the Chihuahua. His untimely death kept the discovery out of medical circles for fifty years. Then, in 1905, Dr. Bob M. Hypodermic rediscovered it after reading through Dr. Hernandez's records. Dr. Hypodermic stole the idea and selfishly named it after himself. But I digress.

Second, if you examine the evolutionary tree, you will see that Chihuahuas and rats are in fact the same animal. Now, Brian, I ask you: If it were twenty starving rats instead of Chihuahuas, wouldn't you reconsider your decision?

The final result: One Rottweiler torn to shreds. The remains are sent across the border to a Taco Bell in your local neighborhood.

BRIAN: Well, Steve, thanks for that little lesson in make-believe history. Did I ever tell you the story about when Wolfgang Rottweiler singlehandedly disarmed the Prussian army? Or how Saint Ferdinand Bernard saved a Swiss village from an avalanche despite being completely tanked?

But back in the real world, these little Mexican toys are nothing but live Milk Bones to that Rottweiler. I mean, what do you think to yourself when you look at a Chihuahua? You think, "My goodness! How do those eyes stay in there?" All the Rottie has to do is poke the little guys and their eyes'll pop right out of their heads. Half of them are probably blinded from the spoon thumpings already.

Face it, Steve, there's no way the Chihuahuas pull this off. A Rottweiler's weight in wolverines, yes. A Rottweiler's weight in fire ants, probably. Maybe even a Rottweiler's weight in chinchillas, but never Chihuahuas. I'm willing to bank the entire Mexican economy or lunch at Taco Viva™ (whatever is worth more) on this one.

Disclaimer: No animals were caged, thumped, mauled, wagered on, or covered in condiments in the writing of this match.

THE OUTCOME

The Rottweiler (56%) eats the Chihuahuas (44%).

THE PEANUT GALLERY™

so, my engineer mind unable to leave any question unanswered, i turned the harsh light of the scientific method onto the problem. by using the two hairy-chested bitches i share my home with as test subjects, i was able to make the following observations:

1. after numerous trials of an experiment i named "fetch," i observed that dogs are essentially single-objective entities. they simply do not deal well with multiple objects in motion. i believe that this is the fundamental factor in why so many dogs suck at juggling. the chihuahuas will have one object to focus on, while the rottweiler will have many.

2. when I went from one dog to two, i noticed that the two dogs did approximately four times as much damage to my home as the one dog alone. i conclude that there is some kind of square law when dealing with multiple canines. therefore, the rottie would be facing an effective chihuahua weight of 24^2 * 5 lbs. = 2880 lbs.

i think that not only would the rottie be obliterated, but quite possibly the greater tijuana area.

Rottweilers:
   Known for: viciousness, bad temper, large sharp teeth
   Owners sued for: The dog ripped apart somebody's face or
      took a bite out of one of their limbs
   Names like: Spike, Killer
Chihuahuas:
   Known for: excessive yipping, peeing
   Owners sued for: yellow stains on the rug
   Names like: Pootsie, Cutsie-wootsie

—Some Dork

In a fierce war such as the one between the Rottweiler and the Chihuahuas, it's best to examine the background of the combatants. First, the Rottweiler. This fine breed finds its roots in Germany, a state known for its rabid militarism and strength. This Teutonic warrior beast comes from a long line of animals whose sole purpose is to consume mammalian flesh (which explains why one never finds a Rottweiler eating at Taco Hell™). Furthermore, the Rottweiler pursues his prey with a relentless fury not unlike the fearsome Nazi™ and Prussian™ war machines of history. To the Rottweiler, the Chihuahuas are just another lesser creature standing between the Germanic canine and domination of the Mexican countryside. Also, let's reflect on how our fair Rottweiler made his way to the dusty backroads of Mexico. Simple—he is a descendant of the killing animals that made their way to South America with Adolf Hitler™ when he escaped from Germany at the end of

World War II. Abandoned by their since-dead master and his clones, this Rottweiler comes from a long line of destructive machines that have had to fight for survival, isolated and alone against an entire nation with nothing to sustain them but the meager skinny flesh of hollow-eyed third world people. Thus, the Chihuahuas are just a means to a larger end—the resurrection of the Third Reich, but this time man's best friend becomes man's worst nightmare.

—*Rod the Bod*

Suddenly the Rottweiler stands on its back legs. Paralyzed by fear, the paying customers are unable to flee as the large dog transforms into: SNOOP DOGGY DOGG. Snoop grabs his Uzi. After mercilessly gunning down the paying customers, he beats the employees to death with a wooden spoon. The Chihuahuas then transform into twenty-four fabulously fine females for an incredible night of partying.

—*Paul Golba*

The Six Million Dollar Man vs. Robocop

THE SETTING

It is the twenty-first century. The ozone layer has been depleted; global warming is taking its toll on the earth's surface; thick smog has become a way of life. Crime has skyrocketed, of course, leading to the construction of a tremendous maximum security prison encompassing what was once known as New York City. In Detroit, there is only one protector: Robocop. His futuristic brand of vigilante destruction is the only thing keeping society together. But is it right?

On the outskirts of the city lie the long since abandoned buildings of the now defunct Office of Scientific Intelligence™. In a sub-basement, a cryogenic freezer fails, and Steve Austin is awakened. Using his Bionic Recuperative Powers™ and a cup of java, he is quickly back to full strength. He emerges from the frozen tomb that long-since-dead network executives had banished him to after the negative Nielsen ratings of "Bionic Ever After." As he enters the city, he spots Robocop, shooting up a car full of drug dealers. The car, now out of control, crashes into a crowded restaurant and explodes. Robocop, unremorseful, continues on patrol. Austin decides that this type of law enforcement has no place in HIS society. . . .

Robocop, spotting an angry man coming at him at sixty-plus miles per hour, assumes he is a criminal and attempts to destroy him. Which "do-gooder" is left standing?

THE COMMENTARY

STEVE: After careful consideration, the Six Million Dollar Man and the 70s greatness he represents will emerge victorious in this battle. True, there are several major advantages in Robocop's favor, such as armor plating and weaponry, but if we delve beneath the obvious, it will become clear that six million dollars will buy a lot, even today.

One serious problem Robocop has is a screwed-up head. Most of the time, he can't think straight, and when he can, he becomes suicidal or remorseful. When his brain isn't working, the IBM-PC in his head controls things, with no chance for creativity which will be necessary to defeat the Bionic Man. Another drawback Robocop has is his speed. Sure he's tough, but he's also slower than Lurch. Steve Austin will be able to juke left and right, evading any attack Robocop might muster.

Steve Austin has the best military, commando, and spy training the good ol' USA can provide. He can do it all, and with a clear head. He can even beat up Bigfoot. If you notice, Robocop only wins against drug dealers and executives, rarely against trained adversaries. He had trouble with ED-209, a lousy second-rate piece of junk. The way I see it, Austin will serpentine up to Robocop at sixty-plus miles per hour and lay a bionic kick right in Robo's unprotected face, reducing his brain to a pile of useless jelly and microchips. Robo will never know what hit him. Austin in ten seconds.

BRIAN: You so quickly look past the "obvious" and fail to realize its significance. It sounds like your entire argument is based on Robocop's minimal amount of exposed skin. I hardly think that that serves as an Achilles' heel in this scenario. Let's look at what both competitors bring to the table. Austin brings speed and strength and a human mind. Robocop brings armor, tremendous firepower, strength, and computer logic (NOT an IBM, by the way). Where is the deficiency in this match-up? It's in Austin's inability to do ANYTHING to Robocop. "Lay a bionic kick" in Robocop's face? Is that the best you can do? Obviously Robocop can deter such daring assaults with his massive firepower. What else does the Bionic Man have to offer? True, in the later made-for-TV movies, Austin did get improved weaponry, like that cheesy laser. But considering those were created for TV movies, they certainly were too cheap to survive the fifty years of cryofreeze.

The way I see it, the Bionic Man, in his anger, is running straight at Robocop in the open street. Robocop QUICKLY raises his guns and lets it fly (true, Austin is quicker, but Robocop is no Lurch). Austin adjusts and jumps for cover, but Robocop is able to follow him with his fifty rounds per second of fire, blow off Austin's good arm, and riddle his circuitry—he is down. Robocop, finding a bleeding, moaning Bionic Man, puts him out of his misery with a grenade launcher right in the transistor. This time, they will not rebuild him.

STEVE: First of all, a few corrections for you. It *is* an IBM-PC. Watch the movie carefully. When they first turn on Robocop, you can see MS-DOS being loaded up (look for COMMAND.COM). Second, Robocop cannot do anything quickly. I can't think of one instance in the movie where he moves even as fast as a normal person. He's just one slow and dumb cop.

I'm glad you brought up weapons. First, Steve Austin has the eye laser you mentioned. I doubt it could pierce his armor, but it would easily fry Robocop's vision sensor, rendering him blind as well as dumb and slow. Also, at the same time he got the laser, Rudy Wells also put in a link between his bionic eye and bionic arm. He has the same targeting capability as Robocop! Steve could pick up an off-the-shelf .44 Magnum (the most powerful handgun in the world) and blow Robocop's head *clean* off. Bye-bye, Robocop!

Finally, I bring up one very important last point: sound effects. *The Six Million Dollar Man* has the coolest bionic sound effect you've ever heard. You know when you hear that bionic noise that Steve Austin is going to kick some ass. What does Robocop have? Whiny high-pitched servo-motor noises. Pathetic! I daresay Robocop will flee in terror when he hears the mighty bionics roar!

BRIAN: Steve, I truly believe that you are going insane. No, it IS NOT an IBM-PC. IBM no longer exists! It may be a descendant of the once-great IBM corporation, but as we all know, "The Company" owns everything in this future Detroit. Which brings us to the subtle point I was trying to make which you so obviously missed: Things have changed! This "IBM" is a state-of-the-art twenty-first century computer, far more powerful than the Bionic Man's *transistors*. How can anyone rationally believe that Austin's pitiful 70s electronics (he's got vacuum tubes in his ass, for heaven's sake!) can even begin to compare to, never mind match up with, Robocop's super-computer-of-tomorrow™??!!

And then you rant on and on about all these weapons that we all know the Bionic Man WON'T have. Again, how are cheesy made-for-TV-movie special effects going to make it through fifty years of cryofreeze?! Not gonna happen!

And then you point out the Bionic Man's cool sound effects. Yes, they are cool in their own little retro way. But you fail to recognize Robocop's sound effects: How can anyone hear Austin's "du-nuh-nuh-nuh-nuh-nuh" when Robocop is surrounded by the music of automatic weapons and grenade explosions in THX? Austin might be the sentimental favorite, but he won't stand a chance. He'd be lucky to even get to Robocop in the first place. Once he reaches top speed, those 747-sized, Tony Manero polyester disco lapels of his will lift him right off the ground. And we all know Austin's flying record. He might stay up for a little while, but before long, BOOM: a six-million-dollar ashtray.

THE OUTCOME

Robocop (55%) blasts Steve Austin (45%) back to the 70s.

THE PEANUT GALLERY™

First off, the six-million-dollar apple pie wouldn't last ten minutes in a bad Detroit neighborhood. He'll come out of his cryosleep, pull on one of his all-purpose orange jumpsuits and go out to see the city. Before he even encounters Robocop, he'll have already lost his watch, his wedding ring, and his bionic arm in a street game of three-card monte. Eventually, he'll have lost all of his bionic parts, his classic 70s Adidas, and every last dime he has on him.

Distraught, he will hop off into the slums, where he will first encounter Detroit's metal finest. Warning Robocop of the dangers of cybernetics, the inherent evil of machine replacing man, and the riskiness of television, the Six Million Dollar Man will fall to the ground and weep. Robocop, his head cluttered with GIF files of Jenny McCarthy, his gears grinding from a long patrol, will kindly shoot the '70s icon and continue on his way.

—Tengu:<> (tengu@ix.netcom.com)

Bionic Man, quick and simple. Why, you ask? Simple: motivation. Robocop has his funky weapons and high-tech computers. That, however, is all he has. He can't eat, can't drink, can't smell the flowers, and lacks the necessary, er, organs for more intense physical stimuli. That's right, he's Robo-Eunuch. So, what's the poor bastard got to live for? Shooting people? Good for a while, but eventually adrenaline burnout sets in and then there's no joy in violence anymore. His life becomes a dull, passionless march through time. It's very likely that he's committed suicide long before the 6m man ever wakes up. If he does avoid kervorking himself, he'll lack the motivation to put up any serious fight.

—Rosencrantz

Steve Austin always takes his time, making sure that he has the right bad guy, then double-checks with Oscar Goldman before proceeding. Robocop shoots first and doesn't bother with questions later (or at any other time). Robocop will spot Austin in his 70s-chic polyester plaid suit, will automatically assume he's a six-million-dollar pimp, and will rid Detroit of one more undesirable. Robocop's armor-piercing bullets will easily rip through human flesh and bionic skeleton, leaving a quivering mess that resembles roadkill mixed with an erector set. When it is later discovered that Steve Austin was a good guy, Robocop will be heard to utter something about "crime against fashion."

—HotBranch!

Six Million Dollar Man had cooler and bigger toys than Robocop. Who can forget looking through the eyes of the Bionic Man doll? They are rare. Robocop is still clogging up the 8C clearance aisle at Toys "Я" Us.

—Sam Panico (masamichinoku@geocities.com,
http://www.geocities.com/Athens/9704/index.html)

Problem: whenever Steve Austin does his "da-na-na-na-na-na-na" thing, he moves in slow motion. He is then an easy target for Robocop.

The battle would sound something like this:

Da-na-na-na-na-na- BLAMBLAMBLAMBLAMBLAMBLAM-
BLAMBLAMBLAMBLAMBLAMBLAMBLAMBLAMBLAM-
BLAMBLAMBLAMBLAMBLAMBLAMBLAMBLAMBLAM-
BLAMBLAMBLAMBLAMBLAMBLAMBLAMBLAM-
BLAMBLAMBLAMBLAMBLAMBLAMBLAMBLAM-
BLAMBLAMBLAMBLAMBLAM

—Chris Bird

"Steve Austin, astronaut. A man barely alive . . . "

That's how it began; that's how it's going to end.

—Call me Shane

Microsoft vs. Disney

THE SETTING

In his small, dank basement somewhere on the upper peninsula of Michigan, Cliff Hoffa steadily pecks away at his keyboard. On his personal computer he is cranking out illegal copy after illegal copy of a bootleg program called "Mickey's Windows 98 for Kids." Strewn around the room are yet-to-be-assembled boxes featuring the undeniable images of Mickey Mouse himself as well as the Windows 95 icon. "This thing is making me rich!" he mutters to himself.

Then comes a loud knock at the door. Cliff Hoffa is never heard from again.

A few anonymous witnesses report two sets of what appeared to be "hired goons" removing Mr. Hoffa forcibly from his home, although most of the neighbors deny seeing anything "unusual." Coincidentally, the next day, both

Microsoft and the Disney Corporation file suit claiming that they deserve the $100,000 Hoffa collected in profits.

And thus the legal battle begins. Splitting the money is NOT an option. Only one conglomerate will come away with the ill-gotten funds. But which?

THE COMMENTARY

STEVE: Well, both of these corporate giants are notorious for their vicious legal attacks on those who trespass into their trademarked property. Neither is going to give up without a fight. It's going to be a long, drawn-out battle—even longer than the O.J. proceedings, if that is physically possible. However, in the end, Microsoft's lawyers will get the money.

There are two primary reasons for this. The first is the intrinsic nature of Microsoft's computer business. With their zillions of copies of Windows 95 and Word, they will be able to produce vast amounts of useless legal documents, writs, contracts, precedents, and Legal Hogwash™. Paper company stock prices will skyrocket. The effect will be that the court will be so swamped with useless paperwork that they may just decide it's not worth it to continue fighting. Disney will give up in disgust, unable to counter with truckloads of Mickey Mouse watches and Donald Duck flotation rings.

In addition, it wouldn't surprise me if the courtroom computers themselves use Windows 95. A little-known feature of this OS is that it is unable to process legal documents in which Microsoft loses. Hence, even with a decision against Microsoft, the computers will print out that Microsoft won. Victory to Microsoft!

BRIAN: As usual, Steve, you analyze only half the story. True, the Microsoft barrage of paper will help clog up the legal proceedings. But if we learned ANYTHING from the O.J. Trial™ it was that judges today are becoming more and more intolerant of time-delaying tactics and irrelevant displays; Microsoft's scheme will only push the judge toward Disney's side. Also, courtroom computers are irrelevant. Sure, top-notch southern California courtrooms may have computers, but I don't think the upper peninsula of Michigan is that well stocked (and I don't see this civil trial being moved out of the county). Nothing there but old ladies on those skinny typewriters.

What's the real factor here? Money? No. It's principle. We're talking about $100,000 here! That's peanuts to these guys!! When it comes down to money, Microsoft is the king of evil. Everyone who's ever used a computer knows this. But Bill Gates didn't get where he is with foolish investments; clearly the hundred grand isn't worth the legal costs it would take to get it. Microsoft's efforts will be half-hearted and will fall well short of Disney's. Why? Because Disney is led by principle. They won't stand for the fact that anyone uses their name and image illegally. They once sued the Academy Awards for trademark infringement. That has to be principle, Steve, because Biting The Hand That Feeds You™ is hardly a moneymaking scheme! Disney wins out simply because they want it more, even though they end up losing money in the deal.

STEVE: Brian, you were right about Microsoft being evil. Too right. However, this evil extends so far that Microsoft will indeed win. You see, Bill Gates (the "Head Honcho" of Microsoft) is none other than Satan himself. Elementary numerology has shown that his name contains "666," thus *proving* that he is the devil (see Appendix A, pg. 178). Bill Gates and his lawyers ("minions") will make legal mincemeat out of Disney.

This is not the friendly "Ned Flanders" Satan, and this lawsuit is no simple "Forbidden Donut." Not only does Satan want the money that is rightfully his, but he wants to do away with those do-gooder cartoon characters as well. The Disney characters are known for spreading joy to children. This is something Microsoft cannot stand for. Instead they prefer underhanded acts such as "General Protection Faults" and submoronic children's computer games. It is even possible that Microsoft will attempt an additional lawsuit against Disney, claiming Disney has stolen the "look and feel" of Windows. Gates will not stop until Disney is defeated!

BRIAN: The only thing that little "proof" of yours actually proves, Steve, is that you never should have ordered that Heaven's Gate Video Series. I'll keep with the theme, however, and play Devil's Advocate: let's say that Gates is, in fact, Beelzebub, Lord of the Underworld™. Where your argument falls apart is with the assumption that Satan could actually defeat Disney! The *Omen* movies clearly show that world domination, when attempted by the Prince of Darkness™, is doomed to failure. Disney, however, is already well on its way to world domination. Or maybe their creation of a "World" and a "Land" isn't convincing enough for you? When you consider their recent foothold in Europe it is truly frightening. The worst aspect of all: They control our children. What better way to gain control of the world than with subliminal messages fed to an entire generation through megamovie hits? It'll make *Village of the Damned* look like *Toy Story*. It will be even worse. And when the children begin taking over, Walt Disney himself, whose body has been in deep freeze since his death, will be revived to lead the way to his "Community of Tomorrow" (but this won't be just an "Experimental Prototype"). Surely I can't be the only one who knows about this.

THE OUTCOME

Disney (64%) hammers Microsoft (36%).

THE PEANUT GALLERY™

Rusty: "All rise. The People's Copyright Court™ is now in session. The honorable Judge Wapner is presiding."

Judge Wapner: "I have read the statements for both parties. I will now listen to your arguments."

Bill Gates: "My name is Bill Gates, your honor. I am the founder of Microsoft. One of the plaintiffs in this case."

JW: "Does Disney have anyone present who is able to make a statement?"

Michael Eisner: "Yes, your honor. That would be me. I am Michael Eisner, CEO and annoying busybody™ of Disney, Inc."

JW: "Tell me, Mr. Eisner, why is Disney interested in seizing the assets of the Hoffa estate?"

ME: "Disney wishes to maintain the strictest control over the quality of any product bearing the Disney name. We have the exclusive worldwide rights to crappy products with the Disney name; if anyone else starts to produce crap under our banner, we'll be forced to improve the quality of our products. The loss of our monopoly would reduce attendance at our theme parks and jeopardize development plans for Antarctica Disney."

JW: "Mr. Gates, why is Microsoft staking a claim to Mr. Hoffa's estate?"

BG: "Because Microsoft is a megalomaniacal corporation, wishing to rule the entire software world."

JW: "In English . . . "

BG: "We're assholes, your honor."

JW: "Mr. Eisner, do you have any more arguments to present?"

ME: "Yes, your honor, we do. Disney owns the ABC television network and we have a signed affidavit from the Nielsen family stating that we are 'America's most watched network.'"

JW: "Mr. Gates, do you have anything to add?"

BG: "Your honor, we have reached a deal with the NBC network which is a small stepping stone before we acquire the network outright. Given our imminent network ownership status, we are willing to have this entire suit settled by having Maria Shriver mud-wrestle against Barbara Walters."

JW: "That won't be necessary, I've reached my verdict. The entire Hoffa estate is awarded to CBS because Angela Lansbury gives me a woody"

—HotBranch!

Let's abandon any hope of seeing this thing resolved in the courtroom. The two empires' lawyers, by themselves numbering beyond the comprehension of the most advanced supercomputers, will bring in tons and tons of legal documents, and in so doing create a heap of matter so large that it collapses beneath its own gravity well to form a black hole. Let's give these two conglomerates a big hand for such exemplary work in getting rid of lawyers.

—Rosencrantz

Walt Disney will arise from his "mostly dead" cryogenic slumber (urban myth or no) and proceed to rip off his own arm and beat the piss out of Bill Gates with it. Legality means nothing when some dethawed fascist freak is kicking your ass.

—Tengu:<>

Consider the gall a company needs to copyright two letters of the alphabet and then sue people who use it because it's part of their last name. Only McDonald's, with their *Mc*™, has ever attempted anything like that. Ever heard of McPizza or McShoes or McComputers? NEVER! Even someone named McDonald is afraid to use a *Mc* in their company name because McDonald's McLawyers™ have tried to legally slaughter anyone who has ever attempted it.

Now consider this. Microsoft and Disney sue each other and it's splashed all over the press. The McLawyers™, who are in a really bad mood after losing the infamous "I burned myself with hot coffee between the legs with no cap in a moving car and I need $5 million" case, snap. *MiC*key mouse? *MiC*rosoft? That "i" is an obvious but pathetic attempt to avoid a copyright violation! Within hours, the McLawyers™ are in McCourt™ and McKicking™ McAss™. Disney and Microsoft will be happy if they can stay in business, never mind the $100,000. Meanwhile, Ronald McDonald and Grimace McKick™ Mickey Mouse's and Bill Gates' McButts™. McDonald's claims TOTAL McVICTORY™!

—Paul Golba

Regarding the famous Grudge Match between Microsoft and Disney, I have an observation you might find interesting. I was just visiting Disney's Web site when I saw, at the top of the screen, an ad for Microsoft, of all things! It's obvious they have put aside their differences and are about to crush us all under their iron heel! My God, no one is safe!

—Falc0 (der Mann mit dem Wiener Blut)

Colonel Sanders vs. Orville Redenbacher

THE SETTING

It's two A.M. at the Centerville Town Mall. The food court is mostly abandoned: Taco Bell, Sbarro, and the Greek Freek™ are all closed and securely locked up for the evening, the teenage employees at home snug in their beds. The only light to be seen in this place, aside from the security lights, is coming from one little store that appears to be open for business, except there's no one at the counter. In fact, the only evidence that anyone is even in there are the rustling and banging sounds coming from the back of the store. . . .

About fifty feet directly across from the counter of this mysterious store, more lights come on. A lone figure enters the movie theater concession stand hauling several large bags of popcorn. This old man is used to making and marketing popcorn, but due to cutbacks and a rash of illnesses in his workforce, he has been forced to do deliveries and he is running way behind. As he loads the popcorn into the bin, he hears the banging and clanking about. He sighs to himself, already used to this bizarre display. He turns to wash his hands and then feels a sharp pain in his temple, followed by the feeling of a warm fluid running down his cheek. He tastes it. Grease! He looks down at the floor at the drumstick that has just struck him: Extra crispy! Does this man have no conscience! He turns. "You crazy bastard! That was the last straw!" He quickly fires a box of Jujubes across the food court that strikes the cash register and explodes, gelatin shrapnel scattering across the vinyl floor. So it has begun.

An all-out food court food war ensues between two food icons, each armed with their own repertoire of culinary projectiles: Colonel Sanders armed with everything KFC has to offer vs. Orville Redenbacher armed with what you would find at a typical movie concession stand. Steve, who leaves the mall alive?

THE COMMENTARY

STEVE: Well, it's obvious that Colonel Sanders is going to come out ahead in this war. There are numerous reasons for this. First of all, we can see from the scenario that the good Colonel has really lost it. He's insane and disoriented, probably from smoking too many of the Seven Special Herbs and Spices from the Original Recipe. This gives him an edge, since he will likely feel no pain, akin to the PCP addicts we often see on *Cops* and in the Grudge Match™. He will be able to charge in, unhampered by (possibly unaware of) the streams of Raisinettes that will be showering down upon him.

Another factor is strategy. Don't forget that you're dealing with a colonel here! He knows how to win wars! He will deploy his drumsticks and wings with uncanny foresight. Orville will never know what hit him. In addition, the Colonel has better weapons at his disposal. Orville has only small projectiles, such as popcorn, M&Ms, Skittles, Twizzlers, and jelly beans to fight his war with. The Colonel has whole frozen chickens, Rotisserie Gold kabobs, day-old rock-hard biscuits, and the dreaded Grease Vat™. Orville beware!

BRIAN: The things you claim will be to the "Colonel's" advantage will, in fact, be his undoing. Orville is provided with a cornucopia of debilitating buckshot (as you point out) as well as a few items which can provide serious damage with a single accurate hit, such as a frozen Snickers bar. All of these items can also be hurled across the breadth of the food court. The Colonel's big guns, however, such as the frozen chickens, the kabobs, and the Grease Vat™ are not long range weapons. Clearly, the Colonel will have to go on the offensive.

And that's where it ends. As Sanders makes his way across the floor (at a snail's pace, of course, since he's 206 years old), a kabob in one hand, a frozen chicken in the other, screaming like a banshee the whole way, Orville has ample time to construct and secure a bunker composed entirely of stale bagged popcorn. As Harland is halfway across the floor, the shrapnel from Orville's bombardment has covered the floor, making it extremely dangerous to traverse. My money is that he'd slip on some Good & Plenty and break his hip, but for the sake of argument let's say he makes it across. But he's definitely going to be slowed down even more, giving Orville ample time to prepare.

By the time he finally reaches Orville, he's exhausted and confused, the high from spices 1–4 having worn off. He lunges, but the kabob plunges harmlessly into a popcorn bag. That's when Orville gives him the soda fountain hose. Blinded, the Colonel collapses on the floor, wailing in pain. Mr. Redenbacher then moves towards the nearest stanchion and, after slowly and calmly unhooking the velvet ropes, finishes the job with a blow to the cranium.

STEVE: There is yet another deciding factor here—diet. The Colonel has been dining on protein-rich chicken dinners for years now. Supplemented with carbohydrate-laden biscuits, mashed potatoes, and cole slaw, he will be as healthy as any old-timer could hope for. On the other hand, Orville is the malnourishment poster boy. All he has to eat is popcorn, candy, popcorn, soda, and more popcorn. This junk-food diet will leave him unable to withstand any sort of attack from Colonel "Body by KFC" Sanders.

Here's the way I see this progressing: Orville, maddened by the initial onslaught, will work his way across the Food Court™ to KFC. Armed with handfuls of candy, he will make a valiant effort to defeat the Colonel. However, once he nears the KFC counter, two things will happen: First, he will see the Colonel close-up, and will realize that the Colonel is just a good ol' boy like himself. Second, the herbs and spices hanging in the air will relieve him of anger and hatred. The next thing you know, the two old guys are sitting in the back room, chatting about old times, and generally having a ball. Then, Orville will mention something about his son. This name triggers a flashback in the Colonel to whatever war he fought in, and he will flip out. Before Orville knows what's happening, Orville finds himself impaled with dozens of plastic Sporks. Sanders is victorious!

BRIAN: Steve, your remarks make me wonder if it's been YOU smoking some of those special herbs and spices. To assume that these men eat only what they will be throwing this evening? Baseless! And what if they did? Sanders's arteries would be so clogged up with cholesterol he wouldn't be able to move, never mind hurl a drumstick fifty feet. One thing is for sure, though: Orville eats lots of popcorn. What will that do? It will make him the most regular sumbitch you ever did see. How will that affect this fight? It won't. The Colonel will be six feet under before the next trip to the bathroom.

And while the thought of someone impaled on Sporks is appealing, it's not possible. You can't even cut open a Buttermilk Biscuit™ with one of those things. This only demonstrates the lack of appropriate weaponry the Colonel has to work with. He is doomed from the very beginning.

THE OUTCOME

Colonel Sanders (65%) fries Orville Redenbacher (35%).

NOTE: Since this match was written, some disturbing information has come to light. In 1935, Governor Ruby Laffoon made Harland Sanders a Kentucky Colonel in recognition of his contribution to the state's *cuisine*. Thus, Colonel Sanders is not what could be considered a true, war-hardened Colonel. Steve, stating that "nothing seems real anymore," has officially withdrawn his support for the "Colonel."

THE PEANUT GALLERY™

If you compare the effects of frozen chickens vs. Chiclets it is a close match, perhaps even a no call. However, have you ever tried KFC's cole slaw or mashed potatoes or (God forbid) the potato salad? These are truly weapons of mass destruction. All the Colonel has to do is loft a few ladles' worth of side dishes (definitely "long range" weapons) behind the "impenetrable" wall of stale popcorn and Orville will be begging for mercy. In fact, I'm a little nauseous just thinking about the consequences of such a brutal attack.

—*Mike Lorenz (Duke University)*

"The Colonel" is a name that conjures images of stately old men drinking gin and tonics in the Ritz lounge. Orville makes you think of a fat kid in kindergarten eating paste. A lifetime of Hatred™ and Anger™ will bubble up, and Orville will become a human tank, completely unstoppable. Meanwhile, the aggressor will think fondly of gin and tonics, and begin to wander off. This, of course, is a dreadful mistake, and he receives a painful popcorn enema.

—*Lord Axe*

Sanders has an arsenal, all of which is frozen or scalding hot. The hottest item Orville has are "hot" dogs, which are colder than Mrs. Redenbacher's libido. . . .

Redenbacher will be unable to use his weapons with any efficiency, since his gawky attire exposes his fatal "throw-like-a-girl"™ weakness. Sanders will launch wave after wave of scalding hot chickens at the multiplex, each wave burning Redenbacher's skin and sending him into hysterical cries of pain. With Orville writhing on the ground, Sanders knocks his victim unconscious with a frozen chicken, then hangs him from the ceiling using one of the multiplex's velvet ropes.

Sanders has the foresight to encircle his victim's body with the remaining velvet ropes, leaving Redenbacher's body where it hangs, where nobody can get to it. Everybody knows that you can't go beyond the velvet ropes.

—*HotBranch!*

Almost immediately, both realize that they are stone dead and collapse on the floor, pulling the contents of the counters on top of themselves in a vain attempt to remain standing. Then the Grudge Match™ REALLY begins.

Considering that this mall's security, if they actually have security, allows walking corpses to make popped popcorn deliveries at two A.M., I feel safe in assuming that this is one low-rent establishment. If they actually hire exterminators, it probably involves a couple of illegal aliens with baseball bats shouting "AQUI PESTY, PESTY!" This place is probably infested with rats and other vermin. And since this place hasn't been condemned, they are probably hiding and are EXTREMELY hungry.

They have two corpses to choose from. Now which would you eat? The Colonel is covered with "finger-licking good" chicken. I suppose that makes Sanders "finger-eating good." Orville is covered with dry popcorn, tasteless Twizzlers, stale Goobers and six-week-old Milk Duds. Even rats are smart enough to know that's not food. Barring a platoon of army ants going through serious sugar withdrawal, Orville's body should be well preserved the next day to be given another proper burial. As for Colonel Sanders, there won't be enough of him left to fill one of those chicken buckets.

—*Paul Golba*

Mr. Peanut vs. Poppin' Fresh

THE SETTING

It's mid-November in southern California and ad execs and commercial directors are working feverishly to produce the big-budget spots for the upcoming Super Bowl. Planters and Pillsbury execs are ecstatic as they prepare to unveil their newest joint venture: Pecan Pizza Crusts™. The director, complete with puffy pants™, sits down and bellows: "Places everyone! Cue the star!" From one side of the stage comes Mr. Peanut, strutting confidently. From the other side comes Poppin' Fresh.

"What are you doing out here, Peanut? I'm the star of this commercial! You're just the straight man!"

"Excuse me?" Mr. Peanut retorts. "I don't think so, Doughboy. I'm the star here. Get off my stage!"

Clearly, this commercial is not big enough for the both of them.

What commercial icon remains standing after the scuffle for the sixty-second Super Bowl Spotlight™, Steve?

THE COMMENTARY

STEVE: The classy Mr. Peanut is going to win this one for a variety of reasons. First of all, Mr. Peanut has that cane, while Doughboy has no weapon. To paraphrase Tom Clancy, "Armed combat beats unarmed combat any day of the week." Mr. Peanut will beat the yeast out of Poppin' Fresh. Poppin' Fresh may just giggle for a while, but eventually he's going to succumb to Mr. Peanut's blows.

In addition, Mr. Peanut has a hard peanut-shell armor. He's virtually indestructible behind that tough outer skin. Alas, Doughboy is like a fat slug ready to be stepped on in comparison. There is also the training factor. Mr. Peanut (notice how everyone calls him "Mister") has an air of class about him—definitely an aristocrat. Everyone knows that those rich boys always learn some skill like fencing or judo. Poppin' Fresh will be defenseless against this trained foe since he likely has no such skills of his (her?) own. Forecast: Biscuits for dinner tonight!

BRIAN: You, sir, are completely insane. Not slightly screwy or mildly eccentric, but completely insane. To think that "Mr." Peanut (notice Poppin' Fresh doesn't call him "Mister") could even last two seconds with my Doughboy is ludicrous. For one, Peanut's top-heavy. One shove from Poppin' Fresh and he's down for the count ("I've fallen . . . "). Second, he's got no muscle to speak of. Yeah, Doughboy's a bit flabby, but he's got some power under there. Peanut's just a hollow shell with sticks for limbs. Third, just look at him! Top hat, spats, cane, monocle: He's an aristocratic pansy. Sure he fences—with pads all over his body and a cage on his face so he won't hurt himself. He's probably got a Cork On His Fork as well. I'll bet a bagazillion dollars that he plays polo because he doesn't have enough athletic ability to play any other "sport." He's the Prince Charles of the Commercial World.

Poppin' Fresh, though, is the Sumo Champion of the Commercial World. Peanut steps forward and jabs the Doughboy right in the gut with his cane. Poppin' Fresh, of course, laughs in his face. As the cane bounces back out, Peanut is thrown on his butt and his "tough outer skin" shatters on impact. Poppin' Fresh all the way!

STEVE: First of all, we both know that "top-heavy" has nothing to do with it. You also like the Popsicle from the "Let's Go Out to the Kitchen" commercial, and he is even more top-heavy than Mr. Peanut.

Another important factor that comes into play in this contest is that Mr. Peanut has some heavyweights pulling for him upstairs. You can bet that Jimmy Carter is pulling strings to have Mr. Peanut win this battle. Poppin' Fresh has no such backing, and will stand alone against the mighty peanut empires of the world. On second thought, I'm willing to bet that Poppin' Fresh does have *one* friend, the Hamburger Helper Hand. The only way he can help, though, is to act even more cutesy than Poppin' Fresh, and possibly annoy Mr. Peanut to death.

BRIAN: I could sit here and argue about the cast of "Let's Go Out to the Kitchen" all day, but that's not the subject at hand. To clarify, I do like the Popsicle—to take that wimp of a cookie. The Popsicle couldn't hold his own against Poppin' Fresh.

Anyway, the fact that you list Jimmy Carter as an *asset* verifies that you are completely insane. What does Jimmy do? He creates peace everywhere. Israel/Egypt, Haiti, the list goes on. Whenever he is involved in anything even remotely confrontational (e.g., Iran hostage rescues), it's a complete disaster. Carter's interference seals Peanut's fate.

And, finally, I'd like to discuss this monocle of Mr. Peanut's. You see a monocle, what do you think of? 1) The British. Well, Poppin' Fresh is all-American, and you don't have to be a history major to know that Poppin' Fresh's boys have already bailed Peanut's boys out of two world wars. 2) Colonel Klink. Complete ineptitude. So inept, in fact, that he was constantly outwitted by *Richard Dawson*. 'Nuff said.

THE OUTCOME

Poppin' Fresh (53%) cracks Mr. Peanut (47%).

THE PEANUT GALLERY™

Beavis: "Whoa, check it out, Butt-head, it's that fat guy from the tire commercial."

Butt-head: "No, dumbass, that's, like, the Pullsbarney Dough Boy, or something."

Beavis: "Ooooohhhhh, yeeaahh . . . poopin' fresh. WHOA, they're fighting! Check it out, Butt-head."

Butt-head: "Beavis, this is going to be the coolest commercial you have ever seen."

Beavis: "The tazer! Use the tazer!"

Butt-head: "Uhhuh, uhhuh, Mr. Peanut's getting his ass kicked by a fat guy."

Beavis: "Yeah, yeah, kick him in the nads!"

Butt-head: "Peanuts don't have nads, dumbass."

Beavis: "Really? . . . But, if you kick a peanut, you're, like, kicking him in the nuts, but if they don't have nads then you can't kick 'em in the nuts, but he's, like, a peanut so you are kicking him in the nuts, but—" *SMACK! SMACK! SMACK! SMACK! SMACK! SMACK! SMACK! SMACK!*

—*Eric Klinker*

Poppin' Fresh is the ideal man. Successful and wealthy, he always gets the job done with a smile on his face. He knows how to cook, make conversation, and be sensitive. Women can't resist him, illustrated by the fact they can't take their hands off him in his commercials. Once the cameras are off, he *rises* to the occasion and becomes the StudMuffin™, fulfilling the deepest fantasies (cooking and otherwise) of these frustrated housewives. All in all, Poppin' Fresh is the James Bond of the cooking industry.

Mr. Peanut is the exact opposite. Emaciated and using a cane, his body is falling apart. He owns both thick glasses (in this case monocles) that are too weak to help his eyesight and a hearing aid that he constantly forgets to turn on. Always cracking under pressure. Mr. Peanut resembles the stereotypical irrational curmudgeon, best illustrated by Grumpy Old Man of *Saturday Night Live* fame.

Absolutely no contest. Mr. Peanut gets his neck (or whatever his equivalent) broken in two as Poppin' Fresh playfully quips, "Sometimes you feel like a nut"—*SNAP!*—"sometimes you don't!"

—*Paul Golba*

this looks like the classic military match-up of infantry vs. armor. actually, mr. peanut looks like that infamous panzer general, klaus von peanufkt (aka the butcher of roesteadt), who escaped the nuremburg trials and is rumored to be living in argentina. the way i see it, the doughboy will build a bunker of biscuits and cinnamon rolls. mr. peanut will use his superior mobility to run around doughboy's margarine line and wipe out his pathetic allies: the belgian-waffle dancers and the french-pastry backup singers. doughboy will escape defeat by making a miraculous leap across the orchestra pit by launching himself from the dunkin' donuts table (thereafter known as the miracle of dunkin'). as any general knows, tanks are wonderful for making the initial breakthrough of a fortified position, but they lack the flexibility of infantry. after failing to crush doughboy in the initial onslaught, peanut will not have the artillery, air, and infantry support he needs to finish the job. doughboy will win, but his once mighty studio will be in ruins. he will make no commercial. instead, a nike commercial (featuring deion sanders in a baseball uniform), an oscar mayer hot dog commercial, and a betty crocker apple pie commercial will fill the advertising vacuum. sic transit gloria doughboy.

meanwhile, mr. peanut will be arrested by the mossad and whisked away to israel for trial. unfortunately, on the long el al flight to tel aviv, he will be mistaken for an airline snack and eaten, thus escaping justice.

—jeff

KITT vs. Herbie

THE SETTING

In the predawn hours in the outskirts of Las Vegas, the crews are busily preparing their vehicles and making last minute changes for the start of the First Annual Grudge Match Road Rally™. There is a tangible tension in the air as the opponents size each other up and plan strategy for the upcoming thousand-mile Las Vegas to San Lucas endurance ordeal. The course begins on flat desert highways from Vegas to Tijuana. From Tijuana it continues south through Mexico to the southern tip of the Baja along Mexico's treacherous "roads" until it finishes in the city of San Lucas.

There are only two entries expected to provide any competition in this year's race. The first is solo driver Michael Knight at the wheel of the Knight Industries 2000, "KITT." The other entry is driver Dean Jones and his mechanic, Tennessee (who looks surprisingly like Buddy Hackett), who will be driving a modified Volkswagen Beetle, #53 "Herbie." It is rumored that there may be several late entries to the race, including Goliath, CARR, and Mr. Thorndyke. Unfortunately several perennial favorites such as the Duke Boys, Starsky and Hutch, and the Bandit were unable to attend this year's race due to factors beyond their control.

The race is about to begin! So Brian, which car can capture the coveted Copacabana Cup™?

THE COMMENTARY

BRIAN: Is it just me, or is the outcome of this race about as obvious as the ending of a *Scooby-Doo* episode with Sideshow Bob as the villain (". . . those meddling kids . . . ")? First and foremost, KITT has Microjam™, a device so powerful that it has been known to down helicopters. That in and of itself is enough, but since I get paid by the word, I will continue. KITT also has turbo boosters, an indestructible body casing, mind-boggling speed and handling, antilock brakes, optional sun-roof or moonroof, and the cool, calculating voice (and, thus, the cool, calculating mind) of a now-obscure TV doctor.

And what does Herbie have? The cheesy "can't lose" magic possessed only by those entities that have appeared on *The Wonderful World of Disney*? Well, that show was canceled and the magic is dead. If the magic wasn't dead, why would Disney have spent all that money on lame attempts to remake *every-thing* that once worked, either through the current *Wonderful World of Disney* rehashes or through their pitiful attempts at artificial, special-effects-induced magic revival with that *Flubber* remake? "Make a little Flub"? They're desperate!

And what kind of motivation does Herbie have? None! He's too easily distracted to attempt to provide laughs for the unseen audience. Herbie, if not drunk off of Buddy's Irish Coffee, will be chasing Babes from *Baywatch* (gee, where'd they come from?), gambling in Monte Carlo, in the middle of a pie fight with Tony Curtis and Jack Lemmon, or just plain Goin' Bananas™! KITT in seven hours.

STEVE: Brian, your arguments are short-sighted, as usual. First of all, let's look at this Microjam™. You, I, and anyone with an IQ of over sixty knows that Microjam™ is as realistic as Ross Perot ever getting elected. It's a nonfactor. And all KITT's bells and whistles may work fine in the States, but when he hits those Mexican roads, you better believe that Trans-Am suspension is going to limit KITT to about ten mph.

Now, Herbie has all kinds of things going for him. First, he has race experience—both foreign and domestic. He's tasted victory, and likes it. KITT won't even know what a race is. Second, Herbie is *fast*. On the racetrack, Herbie zoomed by all manner of race cars with ease; KITT should be no exception. Third, Herbie has an onboard mechanic. *If* something happens, it can be fixed instantly, if not sooner. Alas, poor Michael won't have his Knight Industries trailer around to help him out when he wrecks KITT (he does this about once a season).

Another factor is Mexico. Do you really think a black Trans-Am is going to make it through the bad sections of Mexico? KITT won't make it past Tijuana before he has no tires, trim, or engine. Forecast: an early lead for KITT, but he won't be finishing. Herbie in seven hours.

BRIAN: Speaking of Perot, that's exactly who you sound like. Whenever faced with a question he needs to avoid answering: "Y'know, Larry, I won't even justify that with a response. The American people don't care about that stuff." It's a dodge. Just like your saying "everyone knows" Microjam is unrealistic.

You dismiss Microjam without justification because you don't understand Microjam. And because you fear Microjam. And because Microjam haunts you, my friend. Wherever you go. Kiev. Buenos Aires. Budapest. Do-be-do-be-doo . . .

And to suggest Tennessee could fix Herbie "instantly if not sooner" is ignorant and foolish. *If* Tennessee's sober (a pretty big "if"), it still takes him forever to fix anything. How much of those Herbie movies was filmed in that garage of his? A lot! Why?! 'Cause he's drunk and slow, that's why! Michael, KITT, and their superior suspension system will cruise over the Mexican offroad at seventy-plus miles per hour. Definitely fast enough after the lead they get from that 250-mile-per-hour burn they lay down on the U.S. highways.

And the citizens won't be a factor here. Yeah, crime might be a problem if: 1) KITT couldn't just drive off himself; and 2) they ever bothered to slow down. But they won't even slow below fifty going through Tijuana. This ain't Clark W. Griswold cruising through East St. Louis! With *Baywatch*, what would Michael need with cheap booze and women?! With KITT's advanced tracking system and great mileage, why would they stop for directions or gas? Again, your arguments are meant only to distract our readers, not to discuss the true subject at hand. KITT is parking in San Lucas just as Herbie is rescuing himself from some comical situation in the lion pavilion at the San Diego Zoo.

STEVE: First of all, Tennessee was quite a mechanic in *The Love Bug*. He welded Herbie's frame while sitting in the back seat in the middle of a race! What skill! Second: I don't fear what doesn't exist. Microjam be damned! Third: Never, ever, underestimate what the Mexicans can do.

And now the *coup de grace* that will seal Herbie's victory. He doesn't have to obey the laws of physics! There's just no getting around that. He can race with himself split in two across the middle, yet neither side falls to the ground (and *still* win the race). He can race around in mine shafts, making hairpin right-angle turns in the dark at seventy miles per hour, and even go up elevator shafts. KITT is always hampered by physics: Herbie doesn't need a wimpy airfoil, KITT does. Herbie doesn't need "Turbo Boost" to go fast, KITT does. Herbie doesn't need sensors and computers, KITT does. The list goes on and on. The end result: Disney magic wins over cheesy effects and bad acting any day!

THE OUTCOME

KITT (56%) speeds past Herbie (44%).

THE PEANUT GALLERY™

Herbie will win because in a long-distance drive through Mexico, any car will take some damage. And when the cars break down and need parts, which is going to be easier to find? Microjam computer chips or a Volkswagen motor? Plus those Mexican *federales* will take one look at KITT and Michael will end up eating cockroaches in some prison cell on trumped-up charges while they confiscate KITT as drug war booty and drive it around drunk shooting into the air until the suspension gives or the tank runs dry.

—paTRICK heSTER

The 80s just keep coming back to haunt us, don't they? And I'll bet that Michael Knight will be thinking just that when that stylish black finish starts baking in the Mexican *sol*. The car will keep getting hotter and hotter as the day goes by (hotter than Pamela Anderson!) until KITT finally admits to Michael that his speedy 2 MHz 6502 is melting, two bolts just expanded and popped out, and the engine casing just burst. And let's face it, even if his car wouldn't turn into a slag heap, Michael Knight without KITT is like the Jackson 5 without Jermaine: they're still cute, but the talent is gone. And of course, all during this time the light Disney colors that Herbie is painted in are reflecting the sun, giving Herbie a blinding glow that will distract the other racers, keep the car cool, and make the local peasants that it passes think that they have just seen a UFO, Jesus, or both.

—*Joshua Galun*

I predict Herbie will win—by a nose, in a backwards spin, with Dean and Potato-nose hanging out the rear windows and someone's clothesline, with clothes flapping, wrapped around it.

—*Randy Holloman*

Here come KITT and Herbie now, with Herbie in the lead! But Herbie's in trouble. He's overloaded! Looks like the combined weight of all the Adorable Mexican Urchins™ he was obliged to pick up during the race, not to mention the Unknown Stash of Diamonds™ he was already carrying, has slowed him to a crawl. Not even ditching Buddy Hackett for Don Knotts a few miles back has made the necessary difference. He's stalling! He's stopped, only inches from the finish line! KITT speeds past and wins! Michael Knight takes the trophy! And Disney executives take Dean Jones out the back of the feed store and hang him from a tree!

—*Robin Shortt (SubGenius Pope of Canberra and Goulburn)*

Boris Yeltsin vs. Ted Kennedy

THE SETTING

June 5th, 1996. It's a sunny day on the Atlantic coast in Chappaquiddick. Ted Kennedy strolls along the shoreline, looking for "nothing in particular," thinking about the upcoming elections. He is frustrated—the Democrats are losing ground, this Whitewater™ thing hasn't helped any; his party needs to sweep those elections or face long-term irrelevance in a smaller government. In his desperation, he has returned to the place where he was helped years ago with another problem. His needs do not go unanswered. With a whiff of brimstone and a puff of smoke, Satan appears before him.

"I, Satan, know of thy dilemma. Since thou hast already sold thy soul to me, thou must work for this one." Satan thinks for a moment, and then continues. "Boris Yeltsin has asked for similar help. Seems some Communist is giving him a bit of a scare in his reelection bid. I was hesitant to help him at first, heaven knows how I feel about Communists, but this doth give me an idea. There shall be a great contest between Boris and thyself to determine who shalt receive mine aid! Since I like thee, Ted, it shall be in thy area of expertise—drinking."

In seconds, Ted, Satan, and Boris are transported to an isolated bar in Nepal. Ted and Boris are seated across from each other at a table. Ted gets ready by loosening his tie, and Boris is noticeably eager to start. The bar is filled with rugged locals donned in yakskins, wagers quickly being made between them. Satan starts the contest: "Begin. Trade drink for drink. Last one conscious wins their election!"

So Brian, who wins this drinking duel for democracy, with the drunkest dealt a devastating defeat?

THE COMMENTARY

BRIAN: I gotta go with the Russian on this one, Steve. He's got everything going for him. First of all, he's Russian. Yeah, Ted's a great drinker by our standards, but Russians (and the Irish) have a much higher standard. Saying Ted could keep up with Boris is like saying the MVP of the Arena Football League could start in the NFL. I don't think so. Second, he's got home field. Nepal is much closer to Russia then it is to Massachusetts. Kennedy is completely out of his element. The bitter cold, the high altitude, the military occupation of Kathmandu that no one talks about: They all favor the Rooskie.

Third, and most important, Yeltsin has desperation on his

side. The election is in a matter of days! If this doesn't work, he's got nowhere else to turn. And if you lose an election in Russia to a Communist, first you drop out of politics, then you drop out of sight. This is last-minute, life-or-death drinking for Boris, and his performance will show it. Kennedy on the other hand, isn't nearly so desperate. There's still months before the election and lots of things could happen. Plus, he's not the only one who can help the Democrats. There are no fewer than three Democrats who still have souls to bargain with. Kennedy is far from the last hope. Plus, he's probably just in this for the free booze. Boris in seventy-five minutes when Ted is slapped silly after fondling Karen Allen.

STEVE: You poorly underestimate the capabilities of Ted Kennedy. First of all, what kind of name is Kennedy? It's Irish! You yourself admit to their drinking prowess. Second, Ted has experience. His liver is a well-honed machine, and his stomach is made of titanium. Decades of drinking have made him virtually immune to the effects of alcohol. If anyone can hold his liquor, it is Kennedy. True, the Russians can drink, but one's nationality alone cannot compete against one of the world's elite drinkers.

Boris also has fatigue going against him. Unlike Kennedy, he is a very busy man, always on the go, running the country. This constant activity has made him exhausted and tired. As soon as those first few drinks hit, he will be unable to stay awake. It will be an easy victory for Kennedy. He will win within fifteen minutes, and will celebrate by dancing the night away with the locals. Satan will have to leave the festivities early to finish building his golden fiddle for his next appointment.

BRIAN: So what if Kennedy is of Irish descent! Big deal! I'm of German descent, but I prefer rum over beer, I hate sauerkraut, and I've never owned a BMW in my life. Both my family and Ted's family have been in this country long enough that any cultural or genetic ties to our ancestors have been completely blended away in that Great Homogenizer we call the Melting Pot™. Ted is an American. And it is by those American standards that you incorrectly call him "one of the world's elite drinkers." When it comes to athletics, business, higher education, freedom, and military strength, America is unsurpassed. But America is a drinking world power like Japan is a basketball world power. By America's standards, Kennedy is phenomenal. By world standards, he is mediocre at best.

Boris, however, is good FOR A RUSSIAN. That puts him among the international elite. And to say he's tired in any way shows that you know nothing of the corrupt nature of Russian politics. He hasn't worked in years. He tried to buy the election outright, but his opponent is shelling out the big bucks as well so Boris had to go higher up. And besides, Boris hasn't been around that long. When did The Wall™ go down? Not too long ago. How long has Ted been around? Thirty, forty years? Ted is the one who is tired and, deep down, I think he's looking for an excuse to retire and grow fat off his pension in Palm Beach. Plus, he's got a nephew who tells him the action's pretty good down there. Boris in a little over an hour, giving Satan just enough time to make that trial in New Hampshire.

STEVE: Are you insinuating that Ted has *actually been working* for the past thirty years? Are you claiming that he will voluntarily give up his last chance to bloat government? I think you need a good healthy dose of reality.

There is another issue that has been brought up in so many matches before, but I can't let it go by when it's so applicable here. Past performance. First, Boris is a Russian. What have we learned from years of cheesy spy movies and Tom Clancy novels? The Russians always lose. We, the Americans (Ted included), are the Good Guys™. We always win. Second, there's the name Boris. The only data available on the past performance of people named "Boris" comes from Rocky and Bullwinkle. That particular Boris was continually defeated by a talking moose and a flying rodent! How pathetic. Boris is doomed to failure, and like it or not, the Democrats are going to be reelected.

THE OUTCOME

Boris Yeltsin (60%) drinks Ted Kennedy (40%)
under the table.

THE PEANUT GALLERY™

This is an easy one. Although Kennedy will put up a valiant effort, Yeltsin will be out in front after the first hour. The two reasons are 1) mass and 2) schooling. Yeltsin has Kennedy by at least thirty pounds—and that is not high-protein American mass, that's thirty pounds of highly absorbent potato mass. He'll be able to soak up the first thirty pounds of alcohol before any has to enter his bloodstream. And that brings us to the second factor: training. Russian children of Boris's generation were given vodka (i.e., straight potato ethanol) in their bottles to fight the pervasive authoritarian ennui of living in Stalin's Worker's Paradise. By the time he was five, not only was he a certified alcoholic, his liver and pancreas were already in a fighting trim that no free-world imbiber could ever hope to attain.

Kennedy has in his favor his long tradition of providing Senate service while snockered, his family roots in Ireland,

and his most important advantage—his enormous head. And we're not talking metaphoric "big head," as in ego (i.e. the famous Kennedy Ego™), but actual large bone-'n'-sinew. The voluminous blood capacity of that towering chunk of skull will allow him to out-drink any other American.

But he can't overcome the mass, length and quality of training, and superb conditioning of the former Head Red. (Who will lose the election even with the Evil One's help.)

—Randy Holloman (xxact@mail.datasys.net)

Since the combatants are meeting on neutral ground (Nepal) one assumes that they will be pounding back equal quantities of the same drink. Which automatically gives the contest to Yeltsin.

So they both drink lots—yeah, but look at what it is that they drink. Ted Kennedy gets drunk off wine spritzers and Pink Ladies. Boris Yeltsin, on the other hand, has spent his entire life drinking RUSSIAN BOOZE.

I once smoked a pack of Russian cigarettes. I mean, American smokes are designed to kill you, but Russian smokes are designed to kill you RIGHT NOW. Similarly, American drinks are designed to make you tipsy, but RUSSIAN BOOZE was scientifically designed with the specific purpose of freeing you once and for all from the pain of living under an oppressive totalitarian state. That Boris Yeltsin is still alive testifies to his supernatural constitution, and points to his eventual victory. So no matter what they end up drinking—from warm yak's whiz to rubbing alcohol—Yeltsin wins because he has the stronger stomach based on his drinking history.

—Thinkmaster General

The decision is a no-brainer when you take the wives into account. Hands down, Teddy's wife is the better of the two. Now, when one considers what drives most men to drink, women are usually at the top of the list. Women just by themselves can lead to this effect, but couple their "womanhood" with ugliness, and I don't care what your heritage is, you'll drink straight vodka and like it!

Boris, God bless him, has to wake up next to that huge whisker-clad woman every day of his life. Not ideal by any stretch of the imagination, and who can blame him for taking a nip of vodka now and again. Teddy, on the other hand, gets Vicki. Now, what (who) would you rather do, drink with your buddies in the Senate, or Vicki? I'll bet Teddy chose Vicki too, and as a result I think he probably is out of practice. His tolerance is nowhere near what it was at the time of the Willie Kennedy Smith trial.

Boris, on the other hand . . . poor Boris, it's not like Jenny Craig has opened up a branch office in Moscow. Nothing is looking up for him, there's no light at the end of the tunnel, and as a result, I'm sure he's been drinking at a constant pace for a while now. His tolerance is at an all time high.

—*Doug Nash (djn@shore.net)*

the warm, wet sensation of the village cur licking his bloated forehead coaxed ted back into consciousness. ted rose from his own pool of vomit and wiped the congealing, half-digested remnants of a wendy's spicy chicken sandwich from his bloodless cheek. as his slippery hands grasped the rough wood of the table edge he thought, "maybe i can pretend i only slipped when i bent over to puke—i'm sure i was only out for a minute." ted lifted his bulk above the edge of the table and was greeted with the amber rays of a new dawn, rising and reflecting off of the virgin-white snows of a high alpine glacier; streaming through the window to be broken among the countless overturned shot glasses and half-empty bottles into a million dazzling sparks. the humiliation of his defeat reached him at the same time as two white-hot daggers of pain seared their way up his optic nerves. his cry of anguish and misery was muffled by a thick, sticky goo gluing his tongue to the roof of his mouth. bile surged from his uneasy stomach and ted bent to relieve the purge. as he bent he spotted through a reddening haze a white slip of paper neatly placed under an empty bottle. the distraction relieved the moment, and ted straightened and grabbed the paper in a clumsy bear-paw grasp. as his vision cleared he made out the perfect, spidery script of boris yeltsin. it read: "you have learned much, young kennedy—but you are not a jedi yet. da svadania, tovarish." "that damn russian stuck me with the check," mumbled the senator, as he slumped toward the floor and back into the welcoming arms of unconsciousness.

—jeff

John McClane vs.
The Death Star

THE SETTING

The admiral has hastily gathered his men and is directing them to apprehend the vigilante wreaking havoc upon his brand-new battle station. "We must capture this renegade before he causes any more trouble on the Death Star. Our first target, Earth, will be in range in twenty-four hours. He must be stopped by then. If we fail, the Emperor will come here and punish us personally."

Behind them they hear a set of blast doors open. The admiral and his legion of stormtroopers turn and see a horrifying sight. There sits Darth Vader, slumped over dead in a chair. He is wearing a Santa hat, and something is written in blood on Darth Vader's black cape. As they unfurl it, the admiral reads the message:

"Ho ho ho. Now I have a light saber!"

So, with Darth Vader out of the picture and the Emperor "far, far away" (thus no Force to speak of), can John McClane stop the Death Star before it reaches Earth?

THE COMMENTARY

BRIAN: McClane in a complete no-brainer, Steve. First, look at the track records: McClane 3–0, Death Star 0–2. Second, it has been well established in the *Star Wars* Trilogy that stormtroopers are completely useless except as cannon fodder. Well, the Admiral and the other officers will be too busy planning the attack on Earth to meddle with the intruder personally, so they will just send stormtroopers. Legion after legion of bumbling, idiotic, fish-in-a-barrel stormtroopers! McClane successfully took out highly trained, professional German terrorists. I think he can handle the pansies in white.

McClane, a master of diversion *and* Hide-'n'-go-Seek™, will be setting off explosions all over the Death Star, blowing out a computer panel here, flaming out some air ducts there. No one will have a clue what's going on ... except for Mr. McClane. The way I see it, McClane runs around for about twenty hours, kills about thirty-seven thousand stormtroopers, suffers injuries which, if inflicted on mere mortals, would require 450 stitches, and still gets enough free time to figure out how the Death Star works, all with the help of a Twinkie-eating police officer back on Earth whom he is communicating with on a souped-up ham radio. After twenty hours, McClane figures out the same chain reaction Achilles' heel the Jedis knew about. After a few hours' work, he sets it off just as the Death Star is preparing to fire. McClane, of course, barely escapes the explosion in a hijacked TIE fighter.

STEVE: Brian, I think you've gone over the edge this time. True, McClane has gotten out of some pretty tight jams, but he has never come close to anything like this before. The Death Star (which *has* been victorious in the past against Alderaan) is just too big for one man to take on without special abilities (like the Force). Honestly, John is a New York City cop. All he knows is coffee, doughnuts, and booze. He has no clue about how tractor beams and reactor cores work. He could possibly figure out the light saber and blast guns, but he could kill stormtroopers all day (and probably will) and still not make a dent in the Death Star. As anyone who has seen *Star Wars* knows, the only way to stop the Death Star is to take out the reactor. Contrary to what you say, John couldn't figure this out on his own, and even if he did there's nothing he could do about it. I don't recall any spare proton torpedoes lying around. Result: Earth destroyed, and John McClane spends the rest of his days hiding from stormtroopers in the garbage compactor.

Also, it's important to note that all of John's coolness will be lost upon the Death Star inhabitants. He can shout "Yippiekaiyay" all he wants, but it won't make a lick of difference. Normally this would alert his enemies to how powerful and cool (even approaching Mentos-level coolness) he is, and make them cower in fear, and force them into doing something stupid. However, the Empire has no idea what "Yippiekaiyay" is, and it's effect will be lost. John loses one of his most powerful abilities, thus ensuring his quick demise.

BRIAN: Poor, naive Steve. You set a trap for yourself. You claim that the Death Star inhabitants wouldn't know how cool McClane was because they wouldn't know what "Yippiekaiyay" meant. Well, something tells me those Germans didn't know what it meant either (perhaps that was the confused look on Hans Gruber's face the first time he heard it). But the Germans still knew how cool he was. And the Empire will as well. How does this work? Because John McClane actually *surpasses* Mentos-level coolness. Thus, nothing can stop him, not bad waiters, not rude drivers, not lost sporting equipment, not escalators, not moon-size implements of destruction. (DOO-WAH!™)

And your other arguments are irrelevant (like you expected me to say anything else). Sorry, but beating up on helpless planets like Alderaan, Druidia, and Basketball doesn't count. Secondly, who says McClane needs proton torpedoes? That's what the Jedis used, but I'm sure it isn't the *only* way to set off that chain reaction, especially from the inside. Here's the way I see it: McClane thinks of the perfect diversion. He hooks up with Special Agent Johnson (no, the other one) to get a space-feed to the Death Star. Within minutes, the Death Star is on-line. And before you know it, half the crew is debating over who would win between a Rottweiler and a Rottweiler's weight in Chihuahuas (whatever those are) while the other half are on newsgroups explaining to Trekkie fans why they'd kick the Borg's sorry butt. Thus, with free rein, McClane easily discovers the ship's layout, puts together a *MacGyver*-esque™ time-delay explosive, and is already halfway home as the Death Star meets its maker.

STEVE: First of all, let me note that it is impossible to surpass Mentos-level coolness, as that is by definition the highest level of coolness possible. It's like going faster than the speed of light—it's an absolute barrier that can't be overcome. Frankly, Brian, it's sad when you have to violate the laws of physics in order to prove your point. Second, yet again you overestimate

McClane's intelligence. Sure, he can kick ass, and has good gut instincts (like any fictional NYC cop). But to even make the comparison between him and MacGyver is sacrilegious! In *Die Hard with a Vengeance,* John was presented with all sorts of riddles and brain teasers. How many did he figure out? Zero. It's a good thing Jules "Zeus" Winnfield was with him, or he would have been dead meat ten minutes into the movie.

One final nail in McClane's coffin is the "bureaucratic desk-driving cop" factor. He simply cannot function without his boss or some other agent telling him "That's not proper procedure" or "You're not in your jurisdiction" or that he's breaking some rule or other. This is what normally motivates him—to do stuff in his no-nonsense kick-ass way, just like Dirty Harry, Axel Foley, and McGarnigle. Without the presence of another good-guy cop for him to piss off, his heart just won't be in the work. Without the motivation, it's an easy victory for the Empire.

THE OUTCOME

John McClane (61%) destroys The Death Star (39%).

THE PEANUT GALLERY™

This is essentially a chemistry problem.

The Death Star: Tends to explode.

John McClane: Tends to cause things to explode.

Sort of like Drew Barrymore versus the Hindenburg, when you take a look at it.

—*Marc Moskowitz (http://carleton.edu/~mmoskowi/)*

With the Death Star preparing to fire on Earth, Mrs. McClane is in danger once again. And for John, this means one thing.

It's killin' time. You will see RAGE™ like you've never seen it before. We're talking mangled stormtroopers, exploding toilets, and a really nasty scene where McClane switches the sugar and the salt in all the Death Star's cafeterias. This one ain't gonna be pretty.

McClane will have 99 percent of his body covered in blood by the time the movie ends, but his wife will still slip him some tongue before the credits roll up the screen.

—Lonny, like a chainsaw set on frappe!

The only real challenge for Bruce Willis's alter ego here is whether he'll eventually run out of clothing to be shredded as he wades through the ranks of the stormtroopers, and shoots/explodes/crashes/destroys everything in his path. Even that would be no real problem, as working sans clothes is apparently a common family pastime in the Willis household. . . .

—Jeff Langcaon (wrkimo@aloha.net)

After an hour of McClane wasting stormtroopers and imperial guards, Boba Fett arrives on the station and finds McClane in the elevator shaft. Each fires off 48,317 shots and takes one hit. McClane gets a flesh wound in the leg, which would require most people to have upwards of two hours of surgery, but he will be able to fix himself up later in the bathroom. Boba Fett gets a dent in his armor. McClane, using New York City cockroach–level intelligence, blasts a hole in the wall and jumps in.

McClane then finds a long shaft and drops a chewing-gum-size wad of plastic explosive down it. The Death Star explodes in a fiery ball. McClane watches the flames come up the shaft before running to the edge of the Death Star and jumping off of it, attached to a 2,000,000,007-foot rope made solely out of shower curtains, and lands back on Earth.

—*Some Dork*

John McClane crawls out of an air vent into the sleeping quarters of none other than The Boy In Black, Darth Vader. Thinking quickly, John loads a videocassette from his bag into the sleeping Sith-Lord's chest module. His person violated, Vader, of course, wakes with a start, but his mind REELS as six hours of *Moonlighting* is downloaded directly into his cybernetic brain. The mounting sexual tension between "Dave" and "Maddie" on the show becomes too much for him to bear, as he hasn't gotten any in YEARS himself, and since the episode where they finally do sleep with each other is not on the tape, Darth is denied a release and dies in a convulsing heap on the floor.

After planting a bomb constructed out of freeze-dried ice cream and Tang in the reactor core, John spots the TIE fighter that goes with the keys he found in Vader's room. Hitting the button on the key chain, the hatch opens with a loud *boop-beep-boop* and he clambers inside. As he settles into the padded seats, a French woman he'd rescued from the Death Star brig turns to John, who's starting up the engine.

"Whose spacecraft iz thiz?"

"It's not a spacecraft, baby, it's a custom TIE fighter," John responds.

"Whose custom TIE fighter iz thiz?"

"It's Darth's."

"Who's Darth?"

"Darth's dead, baby. Darth's dead."

—*Isaac Sher*

ALF vs. E.T.

THE SETTING

Midnight. A lone bike flies through the southern California night sky. The bike lands in a driveway. A boy brings a basket to the front door and sets it down. "I'm sorry, buddy," Elliott says. "But one more day and Mulder and Scully would have closed in and taken you away. They'll take care of you here. They can help your kind." With that, Elliott rings the doorbell and rides away.

A tired and confused Mr. Tanner comes to the door. "What is this? . . . Honey! It's another alien!"

A few weeks pass by, and, needless to say, ALF is not happy with the new member of the family. Not only is E.T. being showered with attention, leaving ALF largely ignored, but E.T.

has befriended Lucky and ALF can't get near the tasty furball. Meanwhile, E.T. has figured out that he can modify ALF's spaceship to get himself home. Late one night, E.T. sneaks into the spaceship to steal it and get home, but is shocked to find ALF waiting inside. "Where you going, finger boy?"

"Go . . . home."

"You've already ruined my life here. You're not about to ruin my chances of getting to New Melmac™."

E.T. does not respond. ALF is the only thing between him and a trip home. And E.T. really wants to get home.

So, Steve, who do you like in this extraterrestrial fisticuffs?

THE COMMENTARY

STEVE: E.T. may be the sentimental favorite here, but I have to go with ALF on this one. ALF is an aggressive, don't-take-crap-from-nobody kind of alien. E.T. is a dainty, skittish weasel of an alien, incapable of harming anyone. E.T. would have a better chance of getting home with his record player and Speak & Spell than by defeating ALF. The facts are just too one-sided for there to be any contest.

First, let's look at experience. As of 1998, ALF is 241 years old. At that age, he's seen it all. He's been around the block and knows how to handle himself. And yet with all this experience he's gained over these years, he's still youthful, vigorous, and spirited—ready to take on any opposition E.T. might care to dole out. Alas, naive E.T. generally has no clue about anything on Earth—he can't even speak in complete sentences or land on the planet for five minutes without the military catching up to him, much less defeat ALF.

ALF also has the powerful Muppet Mystique factor working for him. Although ALF is not a true Muppet, any of these pup-peteered creatures is tough and virtually indestructible. ALF combines Miss Piggy toughness, Kermit charm, and Fozzie humor all in one package. Unbeatable! All E.T. has is an extendible neck and a glowing finger. Unfortunately, they won't be doing him any good. After Elliott abandons him, E.T. will turn a sickly pale white and disappear. He'll turn up several days later in a storm drain, after which reporters from the *National Enquirer* will have writing material for a few more weeks.

BRIAN: Hmm. Where to begin. Well, first off, you cite ALF's tremendous age as an *advantage*? You're starting to sound like Bob Dole. At 241 years old, ALF's knees (if he has knees) and other joints are wearing out. He just won't have the moves like he used to. Most people don't know this, but the reason ALF was canceled was not due to low ratings, but due to ALF's dilapidation into senility and incontinence. ALF will be more concerned about adjusting his Depends or yelling at the Best Boy than fighting with E.T.

Second, Muppet Mystique? You got ALF's talents wrong, there, Steve. ALF actually combines Miss Piggy CHARM with Kermit TOUGHNESS. I'll give you the humor of Fozzie, but I wouldn't really take that as a compliment. E.T., on the other hand, is not a Muppet, but a person in a suit. Thus, E.T. can feed off such great powers as the San Diego Chicken, the Philly Phanatic, and King Kong. Talk about charm, humor, and toughness. ALF doesn't stand a chance. E.T.'s zipping home before ALF can even get his spectacles on.

STEVE: Are you sure about that "person in a suit" bit? I thought he was animatronic, in which case he could only feed off the Chuck E. Cheese Pizza Band. If this is the case, I think you'll have to agree that E.T.'s loss is inevitable.

Anyhow, since you failed to present any new and original ideas of your own in your entire argument (instead simply mindlessly bashing mine as you always do), I will present some more food for thought. First, E.T. has that glowing heart when he gets excited. This is too obvious a target for ALF's attack. He just has to reach into E.T.'s chest and do a *Temple of Doom* move to render E.T. instantly dead. Second, E.T. has that all-too-vulnerable neck. Really, could you ask for a better neck to strangle? And those huge cutesy eyes are also an easy target. E.T. has stumpy legs, so he will be unable to run away. Kind of makes you wonder how something like E.T. ever successfully evolved. ALF will destroy E.T., no doubt.

BRIAN: *Yes*, E.T. was a person in a suit. She became a bit of a celebrity afterwards, if I recall. (True, there were some scenes in the movie where they used an animatronic E.T., but that could be thought of as a "stunt double.") Regardless, the Chuck E. Cheese Mystique is nothing to sneeze at.

Oh, and you want an original and new idea of my own? I didn't want to have to point out the obvious, but here goes: E.T.'s got the Magic. If he has the power to heal, he has the power to destroy. If he can make a bike fly, he can make ALF fly. And what does ALF have going for him? Fur. That's it. Well, he could probably win a Barry Manilow lookalike contest, but other than that, he's got nothing. And you try to play him up like some superpowerful high priest. In the words of the great contemporary poet LL Cool J, "No, I don't think so."

When the two come face-to-face, ALF charges E.T. with that hippety-hoppety Muppet motion. Unaffected, E.T. raises his finger and says, "Flooooaaaat." Up goes ALF, levitating off the ground (which reveals that despite the fact his fur stops at his waist line, he's not wearing any clothes. Shudder). A helpless

ALF is floated out of the spaceship and into the nearest Dumpster. E.T. drops it into overdrive and speeds home. Another happy ending.

THE OUTCOME

ALF (66%) defeats E.T. (34%).

THE PEANUT GALLERY™

Genetics will win out in this case. E.T.'s father is another famous space alien, Mr. T. No son/daughter/whatever offspring of Mr. is going to be a wimp. T family tradition will not allow it. Mr. has trained his offspring since before birth to fight, like in *Rocky III*. If little E was a wimp, he would not have survived his father's training. E.T. may have big cute eyes, but those eyes are the Eyes of the Tiger™.

E.T. responds "Pity . . . fool . . . who . . . touch . . . ship. . . . Pity . . . the . . . fool!"

ALF, who can't even take a pampered house cat in a fight, gamely puts up his dukes, too late to protect his big nose. Using the boxing and street fighting skills his father has instilled in him, E.T. starts to turn ALF from an Alien Life Form into an Alien Throw Rug.

—*Craig Denison*

ALF's a predatory animal. Every day, he's up early, chasing the cat like Rocky jogging down the back alleys of Philly. All E.T. does is hide out in Drew Barrymore's room, posed as a toy, watching her get dressed. E.T.'s soft. No regimen at all. Easily distracted. When did E.T. ever display anything resembling a simple reflex action? He's on a slab in a giant Ziploc bag for at least a third of the movie, kids subdue him and cross-dress him, he puts up no fight at all. Plus, Reese's Pieces aren't exactly your Mega-Carbo Weight Gain 9000 from GNC. And if I remember correctly, E.T. was even seen with Michael Jackson, the other eighties superstar alien freak. End of story.

—*George Campbell (caffeine@worldnet.att.net)*

ALF, an ace bouillabaisseball pitcher back on Melmac, launches [a bag of] Skittles right at E.T.'s head. As soon as it hits, the bag breaks open and throws the Skittles out in a wide arc. "Reeesess Piecesss" croaks E.T., mistaking the two topologically equivalent snack foods in the subdued lighting of ALF's spacecraft. As soon as E.T. drops to his knees in search of the candy, ALF jumps him and puts E.T. in his patented "Shumway Sleeper." E.T., realizing the ruse, cries out in terror, then snaps his fingers . . .

. . . and ALF finds himself at the mercy of one of E.T.'s original "fly girls," Drew Barrymore. Yes, it was E.T., small, glowing-heart E.T., barely able to master the high five, who was responsible for corrupting her, and she still comes around whenever she needs his "healing touch." While Drew pins ALF to the bulkhead, E.T. briefly debates between getting reacquainted with Barrymore and showing ALF "The Other Finger." But time is a-wastin'. He has ALF bound and gagged in the corner before he dismisses Barrymore with a cursory snap of his fingers, then sets to work bringing aboard his most prized possessions: a year's supply of Reese's Pieces and 1200 copies of "E.T. Phone Home" cartridges for the Atari 800. E.T. speeds away from the Earth to rendezvous with the mother ship, parked just outside of the solar system.

—*Dave C.*

Scooby-Doo vs. *The X-Files*

THE SETTING

"Freddie, we're lost again!"

"Don't worry, Daphne. I'll just stop by this old abandoned amusement park and ask for directions."

Fred, Daphne, and the rest of the *Mystery Machine* gang venture forth to the park. There they meet Mr. Withers, the park's caretaker. However, instead of giving them directions, Mr. Withers tells them about the recent mysterious deaths and sightings of hideous monsters at the park. Suddenly, from around the corner, two shadows approach.

"Zoinks!* The Monsters! H-h-h-here they come now! Run for your life, Scoob!" Shaggy and Scooby tremble in fear and then run into the nearest tent. As the figures approach, it becomes clear that they are not monsters, but a professionally dressed man and woman.

The man flashes a badge. "Mr. Withers, I'm Agent Mulder, this is Agent Scully. We're here to investigate the recent mysterious deaths at this abandoned amusement park."

Velma exclaims, "Hey, Fred, why don't we also try and figure out what's going on here?"

Fred's eyes light up. "Velma, that's a great idea! We'll see if we can figure it out before the agents do!"

So, Brian, who unravels the mysterious occurrences at the amusement park first?

THE COMMENTARY

BRIAN: The way I see it, two things could happen, and either way the *X-Files* pair win in a rout. Option #1: The mysterious occurrences at the amusement park are due to some paranormal, superhuman, extraterrestrial, and/or mystic force or entity. If that's the case, Scooby, et al., are completely out of their league. They can't handle real ghosts: Scoob and Shaggy would run, Daphne would scream and ask Fred to hold her close, Fred would pee in his pants, and Velma would try to explain what was really happening right up until she was eaten alive, melted, fried, and/or transmogrified. Mulder and Scully, however, are old hat at stuff like this.

Option #2: The deaths and monsters have all been faked so that an unknown person, who has already been introduced as

---

*There is some discrepancy whether this is *Zoiks* or *Zoinks*. It is left up to the reader to decide.

a character, may exact revenge on another previously intro-duced character and/or reap financial rewards. Since we've only had one character introduced, this would mean Mr. Withers is behind it all and stands to make a hefty profit from this charade. With Option #2, Scooby & Co. have a chance, but we all know it would take five to ten minutes for them to solve the mystery. Your first reaction may be, "Well, it takes Mulder and Scully a full hour." True, but that is when they're up against a REAL mystery, like previously unknown diseases, voodoo curses, psychic powers, and/or unexplained weather balloon sightings in southeastern New Mexico. Faced with something as phony as this, it would be over in seconds. Before Scooby gets his first Scooby-Snack, Mulder has already run a background check and an all-too-extensive body cavity search on Mr. Withers. His ties to the owner of the park are discovered, and it's all over. When Scooby and Shaggy are run-ning all around the House of Mirrors in a precursor to the complicated series of events that should lead to the bad guy's capture, Mr. Withers is being led away in shackles. Not even enough material for an *X-Files* promo.

STEVE: Your whole premise of these two options is totally ridiculous. It's not an issue of whether the monsters are para-normal or not; it's an issue of what the *Scooby-Doo* gang *thinks* they are. And we know that they *always* think they're real, especially Shaggy and Scooby. The truth is never revealed until the "unmasking" at the end of the episode. In fact, Scooby and Shaggy always inadvertently capture the baddies *with the full belief that they are genuine monsters*!

You are correct in saying that Scooby & Co. could solve this in five to ten minutes. However, Mulder and Scully will still take their full hour to figure this out. Why? Two reasons. First, there is the obvious FOX Factor™, where they have to milk every last advertising dollar out of the viewers by keeping them suspensefully hanging during commercial breaks. FOX needs a full hour to do this properly. We all know there is no real suspense in *Scooby-Doo*, and no one watches it anymore, so there are no advertising dollars to milk out of it either. Thus, there's no motivation to drag out the solution to the murders. Second, there is the sexual tension issue. In *Scooby-Doo*, there are two men and two women, but absolutely no sexual tension. However, in *The X-Files*, there is the underlying unspoken attraction between Mulder and Scully. The development of sexual tension takes a great deal of effort, and time needs to be allocated for the relationship between these two to develop. While Mulder and Scully are working in close quarters, repressing their desires, Scooby captures the bad guys in a series of zany antics.

BRIAN: Okay, let me get this straight. Shaggy is exploring some spooky basement, and the lights go out. He gets real nervous; he calls for Scooby and hears some strange noise. "Oh, there you are, Scoob." The lights come back on to reveal the Swamp Thing/Shark God/Rabid Mummy right behind him. Shaggy takes his hand (without looking of course). "I think I see a way out of here, Scoob." Just then, Shaggy realizes that it's not Scooby and turns around to see the monster face-to-face. Now, with your logic, by Shaggy simply *believing* that this monster is real, the predictable will happen: Shaggy will say "Zoinks," stammer and panic, and then finally run away (all the while the monster does nothing but growl). Well, I say this only happens if the monster is not real (like in all the episodes) REGARDLESS of what Shaggy THINKS. If the monster IS real, Shaggy is going up to the Spirit in the Sky™

(regardless of what he *thinks*). Your theories make no sense and only help to validate my previous platform that Mulder and Scully win this with real or unreal monsters.

And as far as your sexual tension arguments, you obviously know nothing about that department. Yes, there is attraction between Mulder and Scully, but it's an intellect-based attraction. They get hot for each other when they solve Jumbles™, not when one of them wears tight clothing. If the monsters aren't real, they won't even have to think for more than five seconds, thus no tension. If the monsters are real, there is a chance for tension, but it won't matter 'cause Scooby and pals will be headed to the Great Beyond™.

STEVE: Ahh, the classic Shaggy moments. They never get old, do they!

For the record, I would like to point out that Mulder and Scully are quite overrated. I've seen them do some really stupid things. For instance, one time they tracked this pituitary-gland-sucking mutant (who had already killed several people) into (you guessed it) a deserted construction site, at night. What do they do? Call for backup? Turn the lights on? Surround the site? No, of course not. They go right inside, where the mutant is waiting for them. Mulder gets incapacitated right away, and Scully just barely saves them from certain pituitary doom. Not the smartest moves I've ever seen. They kind of remind me of that stupid family in *Poltergeist*. When freaky things start happening like that, get out! Get some help!

Meanwhile, Fred, Velma, and Daphne *intelligently* construct a trap for the bad guys using an old fishing net, a washing machine, and some roller skates. Shaggy and Scooby are the bait, as usual. Of course, things go haywire, and Shaggy and Scooby end up captured in their own trap. But in the process, the bad guys are also caught, and Fred unmasks them, solving the crime in five action-filled minutes. Top that, Mulder.

THE OUTCOME

The X-Files (53%) out-meddles *Scooby-Doo* (47%).

THE PEANUT GALLERY™

Our *foX-Files* agents have a two-pronged M.O. Scully is convinced that the monsters are no more than a few crackpots dressed up in Swamp Lagoon Halloween outfits (what other explanation could there be?), while Mulder insists that he has finally found the infamous swamp monster that has kept all the locals at home nights for the past century. Once Mulder starts hanging out in the marsh, covering himself in mud and reeds, getting accustomed to the psychic patterns of the beast, the murderer finds Scully alone in the park's office, poring over the financial records. A muffled cry for help comes over the walkie-talkie, and Mulder somehow shows up just in time to shoot the creature in the back as it is about to chew through Scully's neck. As it slumps to the floor, Mr. Withers's face is visible through the Swamp Mask's eyeholes. You hear him faintly mutter, "Damn FBI agents! Those kids never had guns. . . ."

Meanwhile, the gang has been busy looking for Scooby and Shaggy, who got themselves stuck on the Ferris wheel and got it started going at about seventy-five miles per hour. The moral is: FBI agents get firepower. Cartoon characters don't.

—*Cecil DeTurtell*

Scooby-Doo is a cartoon. Therefore, things like random decapitation and skin-flaying are easily laughed off. Hell, I've seen cartoon characters have their still-beating hearts ripped out of their chests and come back after a word from the sponsors. Let's see *that* on *The X-Files*.

—*Joe Valenzuela*

Mulder: Analytical genius, can handle the existence of the supernatural and fake monsters, has a legion of female fans, Oxford-trained psychologist and a brilliantly intuitive investigator.
Fred: Wears a scarf. Drives the van.

The male section is obviously a no-brainer (in Shaggy and Scooby's case, literally true). Mulder has a clear advantage. In the case of the female contingent we have more competition.

Velma: The brains of the outfit, with a sharp mind and a belief in the rational explanation (even though she runs from the monsters too).
Daphne: The body of the outfit. She . . . well, she wears a scarf too. And she has red hair.
Scully: She has a sharp mind and a belief in the rational explanation. She has red hair. She shoots the monsters.

Based on the fact that Scully combines the best attributes of the two others and has the added Rambette factor, the FBI wins again.

—*Keith Morrison*

I would like to comment on issue of sexual tension. Velma, being a lesbian, is naturally attracted to Daphne. Daphne, on the other hand, can't get enough of Fred. Fred, unfortunately, is gay, but covers up his attraction to Shaggy with his patronizing attitude. Shaggy is simply too high on pot to notice anything, and spends his time satisfying his munchies and believing that Scooby can talk.

—Mike Chock (mike@softwarezone.com)

Upon hearing Scooby speak, albeit in a tongue that only remotely resembles English, Mulder and Scully will lose all interest in solving any mystery. Mulder begins studying Scooby in order to determine if his hyper-canine intelligence is the product of a government experiment to turn dogs into obedient soldiers, or an alien experiment to make dogs the dominant life form on earth, thus paving the way for an easy takeover of earth. Scully will attempt to rush Scooby to the FBI HQ in D.C. for an intensive autopsy in order to prove that he's nothing more than a random mutation. With both Mulder and Scully distracted, the gang is free to solve the mystery.

—Mac

While Scooby and Shaggy, cleverly disguised as beauty parlor workers, perform complete makeovers on the unsuspecting Scully and Mulder, Daphne, Fred, and Velma could be off on the trail of the fiendish Mr. Withers. This five-to-two advantage (four-to-two if Velma loses her glasses and crawls off to find them) is the deciding factor.

—Scott

Did it occur to you that *X-Files* agents are at a disadvantage based on the setting? It has the guy at the popcorn stand. The popcorn is being used to smuggle rare minerals out of the country in salt packets. The *X-Files* agents will assume that the mineral traces in their popcorn are from transmutated blood and check at the blood pressure test booth. The gang will check old newspapers from Dumpsters and find enough clues to crack the case before the agents even find the booth.

—*Michael Moon*

The gang will go looking around the swamp (there is always a swamp on *Scooby-Doo*) and find the usual glowing muddy footprints that are always there leading into the amusement park. The gang of course splits up (Fred, Daphne, Velma; Shaggy, Scooby) and tries to find the monster. Shaggy and Scooby of course run into the monster and after a long chase somehow manage to capture it. The whole group (now reunited) gather around the creature to unmask it. Unfortunately for them, they realize too late that it is a REAL monster (some kind of inbred alien Neanderthal/Lamprey that has a taste for human livers and is on the payroll of the CIA).

Two minutes later, Mulder and Scully, who have been conducting a thorough investigation and know exactly what they are up against, burst in with a fully armed SWAT team only to find a blood-splattered room with three clues in the center: a pair of glasses, glowing muddy footprints leading to the swamp, and an empty box of Scooby Snacks.

. . . Two weeks later, in a darkened room in Washington, D.C., a man, surrounded by a halo of smoke, sits talking on the phone. "Excellent work, Withers, you managed to keep Mulder busy and out of our way with your little pet" . . . pause . . . "Oh, really? Good! We finally got rid of those meddling kids and their dog."

—*Amish Commando*

Ellen Ripley vs. Sarah Connor

THE SETTING

The sound of Tina Turner's voice fills the air as the hordes of cheering postapocalyptic masses hover around the Thunderdome for tonight's special event. The Thunderdome has been specially outfitted tonight with flamethrowers, knives, chains, whips, and all manner of weapons (sorry, no firearms). The two contestants are escorted into the large geodesic dome amid the bloodthirsty cries of the spectators. The contestants look each other over and make mental notes of the weapons scattered around the dome. The crowd goes silent as Tina Turner speaks:

"We have a great fight for you tonight! First, brought to you all the way from Los Angeles, "The Terminator Terminator," Sarah Connor! And her opponent, from the deepest reaches of space, the famous "Alien Killer," Ellen Ripley! Tonight, they will fight to the death!! [*The crowd goes wild.*] Let the fight begin!"

So, Brian, who wins this brutal battle between these brawny babes?

THE COMMENTARY

BRIAN: First of all, let me clarify that this *HAS* to be the buff and tuff *T2* Sarah Connor and not the soft, girl-next-door, "Do you want fries with that?" *T1* Sarah Connor. If it's not, then you might as well put Alice out there, 'cause it wouldn't change matters any. (Alice from the Brady household, Alice from Mel's Diner, Alice in Wonderland, doesn't matter. The *T1* Sarah is in the same flabby class as any of 'em.)

With that being said, let me say that even the buff and tuff *T2* Sarah Connor doesn't stand a chance in hell. Let's look at their track records. Sarah Connor did lots of hiding: behind machinery, behind Ahh-nuld, etc. There is no hiding in the Thunderdome-dome-dome-dome. (*The preceding was an echo effect only available in Grudge Match, Da Audio Book™*). The only times she ever really came out and fought were: 1) against a bunch of psychiatrists and lab technicians—ooooh, impressive; 2) in the final scene against the T-1000. Yes, it was courageous, but all she really did was push him backwards and knock him into a molten pool. She never really killed him herself. And there are no molten pools in the Thunderdome-dome-dome-dome, which, regardless of Connor's past experience, is a good thing for Ripley.

Ripley, on the other hand, just goes out and kicks tail. Yeah, she does some hiding in the beginning of her movies, but that's just for suspense and character development, which aren't factors here. When it comes time to pay the bills, Ripley gets the job done. Did you see her walk right into the heart of that nest and hold the entire Alien colony hostage with her rifle/flamethrower/grenade launcher/salad shooter? Sorry, but with balls like that, no bitch is gonna get in her way.

STEVE: First of all, let me clarify that this *HAS* to be the ruff and tuff *Aliens* Ellen Ripley and not the soft, "Where's my cat," let-me-strip-down-to-my-panties-and-go-hide-in-a-closet *Alien* Ellen Ripley. If it's not, then you might as well put Debbie Gibson or Tiffany out there.

With that being said, let me say that even the ruff and tuff *Aliens* Ripley doesn't stand a chance in hell. Even in *Aliens* she spent the early parts of the movie in a psycho ward, having nightmares and flashbacks to the previous movie. Kind of like those Vietnam flashbacks people are always having in really bad shoot-'em-up movies. In the middle of the fight Ripley would lapse into a nightmare, and then Sarah would quickly move in for the kill.

Sarah Connor, on the other hand, has several things going for her. First, she is honed. Remember her doing chinups in *T2*? I'd like to see Ripley and her flabby physique try that one. Ripley might possibly have a chance in the physical category if she gets possessed by Zuul again, but with no Ghostbusters around to save her, she'd be dead meat anyway. Second, Sarah is extraordinarily crafty and vicious. Her escape from the psycho ward using paperclips, hypodermic needles, and hostages demonstrates this cleverness and ruthlessness. Third, Sarah was trained by ex-commandos living in Mexico (the best ones hide in Mexico, from what I hear). With her superior training and strength, she'll be unbeatable. Finally, since the Terminators have essentially ruined her once peaceful life, she's basically all-around pissed off, which leads to the power of the Rage™. All around, Sarah is going to kick some ass.

BRIAN: Oh, c'mon, Steve. What's Rage™ got to do with it (got to do with it)? What's Rage™ but a secondhand emotion? More meaningless blather. Second, your comments on Ripley's flashbacks and mental stability being a problem are just about to blow up in your face: 1) She didn't really belong in a loony bin. She was put there illegally by the Evil Paul Reiser™. (I don't know who was responsible for the casting on that one, but I'm going to see to it personally that they never work in Hollywood again.) 2) Grudge Match Precedence tells us that flashbacks do not prevent victory (see Rocky v. Rambo). 3) While Ripley may have a flashback or two, Connor is prone to *FLASHFORWARDS*. And not just any flashforwards, but apocalyptic, cataclysmic, wailing-and-gnashing-of-teeth kinda flashforwards. Seconds into the match, Connor will get a vision of her own horribly mangled body hanging by one leg from a tattered bungee cord. She becomes paralyzed with fear and Ripley grabs the Thunderdome Axe™ and liberates Connor's head from the rest of her body.

Another major factor to consider here is adaptability. Neither of these participants have ever been in the Thunderdome before, so who is going to adjust to its nuances quicker? The woman who has never really traveled far from her corner of the world and who looked uneasy in a paper hat? No. It will be the woman who has faced life-and-death adversity on three drastically different backdrops: space freighter, deserted colony, and prison planet. After adjusting to that rock from *Alien³* so easily, taking advantage of the subtleties of the Thunderdome will come secondhand. Sarah Connor will come in trying to be a hero, but we don't need another hero, Steve. We need the experience and the guts which are Ellen Ripley. Or which are any of her clones.

STEVE: Let me correct you on a few issues. First of all, that was not officially the "Evil Paul Reiser." As we all know, in order to qualify as "evil version" of anyone, one must have a goatee. Your so-called "Evil" Paul Reiser was clean-shaven. At worst, he was simply an asshole, but definitely not Evil. Second, Sarah's "flashforwards" will actually help her. Since these mental lapses all occur in the apocalyptic future, and the Thunderdome is in the apocalyptic future, she will be well prepared. Even for Tina Turner's hair.

As far as traveling experience, I assure you that some parts of L.A. are far more scary than any old deserted colony or space freighter. I don't think you give her the credit she deserves for being able to survive in that environment.

Most likely this battle will never come down to weapons. Sarah will just charge Ripley. With her superior strength and training, she will just break Ripley's neck or spine. That will be it. Without a weapon such as a flamethrower, grenade launcher, or hydraulic walking forklift, Ripley simply doesn't have a chance. And Sarah isn't about to give her that chance.

THE OUTCOME

Sarah Connor (57%) terminates Ellen Ripley (43%).

THE PEANUT GALLERY™

I voted for Connor. Man, if I were a security guard, and she were restrained and catatonic, I'd lick her too!

—*David Nelson*

It is my belief that Connor would walk up and promptly break Ripley's neck. However, the unborn alien in Ripley's stomach would then make an untimely appearance and kill the person tormenting its host body. After that the alien would be forced to make a new home in Tina Turner's hair until it was full grown. Chances are she would not even notice.

—*Marsh*

Sarah Connor has only one motivation: John Connor. Her only child is going to save the world from the robot holocaust. He must be kept safe at all costs! For him, she's shacked up with every two-named drunk biker/mercenary she met so they could teach John necessary skills, fought the inept system that thought she was insane, helped defeat two terminators, AND put herself in situations of certain doom to protect her son. Then combine that with being a single mother who alone endured potty training and piles of Mexican diapers, suffered through John's all-night fevers and accidental bullet wounds, and rejoiced at John's first steps and first robbery of an ATM. We are talking serious dedication here!

But, as any mother could tell you, the job is far from over. John has so much left to learn! He must be protected! Who else is there to do that? Foster parents? Will they make sure he brushes and flosses three times a day? Will they get the blood-stains out of his camouflage after a long day on the job? Will they break John out of prison in a daring daytime helicopter raid? Can they teach him how to kill a man instantly with the two scoops of Kellogg's Raisin Bran, part of a full balanced breakfast? Not likely! And we all know what happened the last time a terminator showed up! So, who will be there for him in his time of need? MOM, THAT'S WHO! She must stay alive, dammit, and protect her baby, the fruit of her womb, the child she carried for nine months, the infant she nursed in her arms. And if she has to kill "baldy" to do it, so be it.

I give Sarah thirty seconds before she rips out Ellen's intestines and strangles her to death with them. DON'T MESS WITH MOM!

—Paul Golba

Hmmm . . . This is tougher than it looks, especially since I haven't seen any of the *Alien* trilogy. . . . Because of this, I will be taking big leaps in my analysis. . . .

The hair factor: Linda Hamilton (run of the mill locks) and Sigourney Weaver (the oh-so-hip bald look in *Alien³*). Since Ripley looks a lot like Sinéad O'Connor, or the lead singer of Midnight Oil, I'd have to go with her.

Now going on to outside influences . . . Do you honestly think that the Gatekeeper will lose to one who acted alongside Toonces the Driving Cat? True, you will need nerves of steel with that kooky cat, but having demon-possessed sex with Rick Moranis, hoser extraordinaire, is scarier in my books (even if it was acting . . .).

My prediction: Ellen Ripley in less time than it takes the crowd to sing a rousing rendition of "Beds Are Burning."

—Vlad the Wonder Hamster (http://www.ualberta.ca/~kjago)

I voted for Connor for a very simple reason. I wanted to punish Brian for excessive references to Tina Turner songs.

—Morgan

Waldo vs. Carmen Sandiego

THE SETTING

The Scene: The West Edmonton Mall, a hub of rampant consumerism on a busy Saturday afternoon at the height of the Christmas shopping season. Hordes of square footage filled by over eight hundred stores of redundant goods and services; a monstrosity of retail horror further enhanced by four submarines, a minigolf course, an indoor amusement park, wave pool, water slide, hotel, hockey rink, over a hundred eateries, twenty-thousand-plus parking places, and cross-dimensional nexus for auto parts.

The Buildup: Two mysterious figures are roaming through the crowds contained within the world's largest retail space.

One, dressed in a jaunty red-sweater-and-toque arrangement, whisks past a trench-coat-clad female. Both turn to catch a glimpse of their competitor, but each has already disappeared into the crowd. The conflict begins. Who will emerge unfound?

The Competition: Our two combatants, Carmen Sandiego and the ever-unfindable Waldo, must play a game of hide-and-seek within the confines of the gargantuan space of the West Edmonton Mall. . . . They shall both hide, and the first one to be found by the Terminator T-1000 shall be declared the loser (and terminated).

THE COMMENTARY

BRIAN: Carmen in a laugher, Steve. It all boils down to one thing: henchmen. Waldo's all by himself in this; Carmen's got scores of large, husky henchmen to perform her will. Will these henchmen successfully do battle with the T-1000? No, of course not. Don't be silly. But what they can do is *assist* the T-1000. So what we've got here is the T-1000 looking for Carmen or Waldo, plus about twenty or so henchmen searching for *just* Waldo. Sorry, but the odds are just stacked against him. Carmen hangs out in one of the London Fog dressing cubicles while Waldo is hunted down and killed like the dog he is.

Okay, Waldo does have one chance: if he's so deceptive that even the T-1000 *and* the henchmen can't find him. Well, last time I checked, Waldo stuck out so bad that even a three-year-old could spot him. With that butt-ugly bright red sweater and that goofy hat, he'd be better served wearing a billboard that says I'M WALDO, COME KILL ME. True, it is Canada, so you would expect more goofy hats and ugly sweaters than in the U.S., but he's still gonna be easily spotted. The way I see it, Waldo hides for a while, but then goes back to his nature: dissolving into a crowd of people doing a happy activity. Thus, he lets his guard down and spends a little too long at the NHL-size ice rink™. One of the henchmen spots him and alerts the T-1000, who proceeds posthaste to the rink. Walking past the skate rental booth (why would he need to rent skates?) and pushing aside the ticket taker, he glides across the ice and sends Waldo to that big penalty box in the sky.

STEVE: In your analysis you're forgetting two important points. First, Waldo is in his element. He thrives in the huge unseemly crowd that the West Edmonton Mall is sure to provide. And he won't be as easy to spot as you suggest. First, as you mention, Canada is "the land where toques were born" (oh, and ice too), so the toque will not help you spot him. Second, his red and white colors will be impossible to spot amongst the red Christmas decorations, white plastic snowflakes, and ubiquitous red and white Canadian flags. And a quick look around notes that backpacks and walking sticks are in vogue these days. I daresay that the T-1000 will have an extremely difficult time looking for Waldo. Carmen, however—she will stand out like a sore thumb. With her trench coat and sombrero-size hat she would be more at home in Paris or Rome (or any exotic location), but NOT Edmonton. Easy pickings for the T-1000.

Second, with Waldo's timeless charm comes compassion from the shopping crowds. When T-1000 asks, "Have you seen this boy?" everyone will just shrug their shoulders. They don't want to be responsible for the death of such a Canadian-seeming folk hero. But Carmen is a criminal, and kind of shady-looking too. Everyone will be suspicious of her to begin with, and will turn her in at the first opportunity. As soon as she walks into a store, the manager will think she is going to shoplift something and will call security. Of course, on the other end of the phone won't be security, but instead the T-1000 impersonating one of the security guards. (The actual guard has a five-foot sharpened liquid-metal finger though his skull). T-1000 heads right down and makes quick work of the two-bit hussy.

BRIAN: Once again you set a trap and then waltz right into it. You make a valid point that backpacks and walking sticks are "in vogue" these days. But you forget that this is being held in Canada, which lags behind socially. While Waldo's accessorizing would help him blend in at an American mall, his lack of a butterfly collar or bangle bracelets will serve as a homing device.

And let's discuss further the topic that you lightly dance around: mall security. Carmen is a thief, pure and simple. What does that mean? Two things. One, she'll have no problem stealing clothes and changing in order to disguise her appearance. Waldo, unfortunately for him, has as many wardrobe options as Fred Flintstone or Gilligan. Two, Carmen could purposely get caught stealing things. How will this help her, you ask? It will release an army of over-sixty rent-a-cops, which will completely clog up the works. If the T-1000 sees Carmen, he'll try to go after her, but will find himself stuck behind a line of silver-haired sheriffs moving at a snail's pace. Have you ever tried to get around old people in the mall before? Impossible! And even if he does slice them all in two, there would be a second wave still in his way (just like in *Zulu*). By the time he gets through, Carmen has already hit the water slides.

And besides, everyone knows that every forty-five seconds or so a woman very near Waldo will take off her clothes (to reveal a sexy bikini) and start table dancing. That draws attention. And if that doesn't do it, Eddie's searing guitar solo right in front of Waldo will bring the entire mall to a standstill and serve as a beacon right to our soon-to-be-fallen comrade. Siddown, Waldo.

STEVE: Van Halen's musical antics are not going to be as noticed as you might think. With the T-1000 roaming around, Guns n' Roses' "You Could Be Mine" will be blaring away, greatly detracting from Eddie's videos. The women will flock to see Axl Rose, and thus all the men will follow.

Finally, Waldo will have protection. In a nearby store, Arnold and Sinbad are fighting over Turbo Man when Sinbad wallops Arnold over the head with a baseball bat. This action creates an interesting chain of events. First, Arnold's computer brain is kicked back into Terminator mode. Second, the blow damages some of the data stored in it; instead of protecting John Connor, he now must protect . . . he scans the store for the first boylike person he sees . . . Waldo. Third, Arnold turns around to an aghast Sinbad and grabs him by the ear and throws him through a conveniently placed plate-glass window. With Arnold now on Waldo's side, there's no stopping him! Plus, the remaining shoppers are overjoyed to have Sinbad out of the picture, giving their undying gratitude to Arnold, and thus Waldo as well. With protection like this, Waldo will easily win.

THE OUTCOME

Waldo (54%) says *hasta la vista* to Carmen Sandiego (46%).

THE PEANUT GALLERY™

The T-1000 is going to look awfully conspicuous in Edmonton if he shows up looking like Robert Patrick, in the cop form of T2. He will not look anything like an Edmonton cop, which is to say that he is not A) bald and B) fat. Thankfully, there are legion of donut stores in WEM that he can hang around to get an idea.

Since it is December, one can easily assume that the only people at the mall are locals. Edmonton's a nice place to be in, say, May, but in December it's gonna be forty below and smart tourists will be in Tahiti. The dumb tourists will have frozen to death getting to the mall.

So how does T-1000 disperse the crowd? Simple. He just heads over to the massive video display bank in front of the Brick and puts a copy of *Don Cherry's Rock 'em Sock 'em 8* into the VCR. This will instantly draw all Canadians present into the area to watch the hockey fights, vicious checks, and spearing penalties with assorted *Oooh*s, and *Oh, that's gotta hurt*s. The only two people in the mall not genetically drawn to watch the hockey carnage will be Carmen and Waldo. Who will be the easier for the T-1000 to spot?

Carmen is dressed in trench coat and fedora. Not exactly inconspicuous, but certainly more so than Waldo, who is always standing there facing you, waving and wearing that goofy "Hey, what's goin' on?" grin. While Carmen slips into the London Fog outlet, Waldo continues waving at the T-1000 even as he gets that walking stick implanted where the sun don't shine (Edmonton).

—Thinkmaster General

Carmen's exposure is just too great—with two irritating kids' game shows, books, and about a thousand versions of a com-

131

puter game which are all basically an insidious way of trying to trick unwitting children into thinking they're having fun while they're actually learning, Carmen just draws too much attention to herself. Sure, Waldo's a popular guy, but his media exposure is a coupla books and a cheap-ass Nintendo cartridge that stays tucked firmly in the back of the discount rack at Blockbuster Video.

But Carmen's main downfall is inevitable—Rockapella. Four geeks in loud suits singing in four-part harmony is tough to ignore. From the first melodic strains of "Well, she sneaks around the world, from Berlin to Car-o-li-na . . ." as Carmen frantically urges them to shut up in hushed tones, Carmen's dead meat. The T-1000 auditory sensors pick up the disturbance immediately and home in. Either that, or the other holiday shoppers mob the faithful a cappella group (and Carmen simultaneously) and flog them to death after already being inundated with Muzak disco versions of "O Holy Night" up the wazoo. Either way, the unshakable Rockapella directly causes Carmen's demise. QED.

—JMR (Cornell University)

Carmen has a secret weapon—no one knows what's under the trench coat! As the T-1000 approaches, she flashes him. Whatever is under the coat is good enough to surprise him for a few seconds. The henchmen then throw T-1000 through another handy plate-glass window and into the Canadian winter, which easily reaches liquid nitrogen temps. The T-1000 freezes solid. A few whacks with a Louisville slugger, and the terminator is reduced to ball-bearings. Since he won't thaw back out into liquid for at least eight months (if ever—this is Canada!), Carmen escapes. Waldo, happy to drift forever in the mall crowds, is left to face a defrosted T-1000 now sporting a bad attitude and a splitting headache.

—*Beowulf*

Waldo'll be tossing out little trinkets, books, etc., and will also be magically causing funny little things to happen throughout the mall, like some caveman running around with his loincloth on fire. Now *that's* humor.

Using this devious ploy, Waldo will have little difficulty distracting the T-1000, which we all know will be busy being skinny and grooming his massive, outlandish ears.

On the other hand, there's the feisty Carmen. Admittedly, she does have an army of arch-criminals at her disposal. But have you ever played a Carmen game before? Not only are they caught by munchkin game players all the time, but, when caught, these criminals routinely give up Carmen at the drop of a hat! Carmen's army needs a lesson in loyalty.

—*Matt "Robert Patrick is a wimp" Lynch*

Unlike Waldo, Carmen does have a surname, thereby making her exponentially easier to track, especially as she'd leave a credit history as she drifted around the mall, which would be as easy to follow as an oil spill from a leaking supertanker. Wal, conversely, is a poor backpacker who would sparingly use his meager supply of hard cash. Waldo will be thumbing a lift while Carmen's last gasps are caught by a concerned onlooker: "She said she was going to visit—uh—Rama Krishnu by the Silver Shores of the Celestial City?"

Yes, folks, she's traveled the world, she's tripped through time, now visit the Halls of Valhalla, the Seven levels of Hades, the Happy Hunting Ground, and MORE in *Where in the Afterlife Is Carmen Sandiego?*

—*John Hunter*

A gaggle of tykes, well trained by several Waldo books and innumerable Sunday strips, are shouting "I see him! I see him!" T-1000 follows them to his quarry. Waldo tries desperately to hide, but the children are too eagle-eyed and persistent. Soon, however, they run screaming from the gory spectacle, and Fox buys the security-cam videos of the carnage for a special: *Retail Slaughters II*.

—*Call me Shane*

Waldo could easily win by employing some new tactics. Waldo is always presumed to be in a big crowd, so what he needs to do is go to the store that sells those big belt buckles, cornhusk dolls, and wood-carved name plates. NO ONE will be there. In his solitude, Waldo will have found the perfect hiding place.

—*Vic "I've spent too much time at the mall" Wachter*

Waldo is the epitome of chaos. Everywhere he goes, seemingly normal people begin to act like complete buffoons, vehicles of every sort swerve out of control, edifices of every architecture sway precariously. If the Lord of Chaos can affect all matter, why would he not affect the T-1000? Surely as soon as the T-1000 gets within fifty yards of Waldo he will find himself ducking anvils, coconuts, and the like. Even the T-1000's sophisticated computer cannot track an infinite number of moving objects. So he fixates on the only still object in the room: Carmen—relying on her proven tactic of hiding to elude the T-1000. The security guards are never sure where that red stain on the wall came from.

—*Brian Kutner*

Fact: Everyone (more/less) knows and recognizes Waldo. When the Terminator holds up the photo of Waldo and asks "Have you seen this man?" everyone and anyone who has been within one thousand feet of Waldo will remember it and point the Terminator in the right direction.

Fact: Nobody (more/less) knows or recognizes Carmen Sandiego. When the Terminator holds up the photo of Carmen and asks "Have you seen Carmen Sandiego?" everyone will reply "Who in the world is Carmen Sandiego???"

Fact: Carmen Sandiego is a woman. Women love to shop. When you go to a mall with a woman and split up, you will be sure to spend at least an hour looking for her, followed by two hours sitting on a bench hoping *she finds you*.

Fact: Waldo is a man. Men sit around on benches waiting for women (or Terminators, in this case) to find them.

Fact: My two-year-old cousin can find Waldo in a Waldo Book in a few seconds.

Fact: My two-year-old cousin has not yet been able to finish the *Where in the World Is Carmen Sandiego?* CD-ROM computer game.

Theory: The Terminator can do just about anything my two-year-old cousin can do, and probably more.

Winner: Carmen Sandiego

Prediction: Waldo will be *voted* the winner, just because he is a more recognizable character (which just goes to prove my point).

—*The Grey Man*

Andy Taylor vs.
The Cunninghams

THE SETTING

It's another sunny schoolday afternoon and Richie Cunningham has spent the past several hours throwing down "pop" at the town's teenage watering hole, Al's. Finding a moment between Ralph Malph's bad jokes, Richie gets up to play some pinball. Unfortunately, he doesn't see the fake vomit Ralph left on the floor, slips, and crashes headfirst into the jukebox. Unconscious for several minutes, Richie is finally revived with a snap of the Fonz's fingers.

"Hey, Richie? You all right?" asks a concerned Potsie.

"Yeah, I think so." Richie lies there confused. Not only is he still dazed from the blow, but he also remembers . . .

Later that day the phone rings in the sheriff's office of a small town. A shaky deputy answers. "Hello? Just a minute. Andy! It's for you!"

Two weeks later, Milwaukee District Courtroom. Opening statements are about to begin in the custody battle over Richie Cunningham/Opie Taylor. Andy Griffith will argue that he is the biological father and that, along with Aunt Bee, he would provide a better home for little Opie. He will also accuse the Cunninghams of kidnapping and brainwashing Opie. The Cunninghams will argue that they are in fact the rightful and better parents. They will claim that Richie's flashbacks are artificial memories implanted from watching too much TBS as a child. Unfortunately, neither side can produce any concrete evidence such as a birth certificate.

Due to flu season, the judge pool is extremely depleted. The only available judge with child custody experience is King Solomon, who will preside over today's proceedings. To whom will the ever-wise Solomon award custody? Under obscure state laws, joint custody or splitting Ron Howard in two are not allowable options.

THE COMMENTARY

STEVE: Well, Brian, I'm afraid Mr. and Mrs. C are in for some disappointment. Richie is going to revert to being Opie Taylor under state law. There are many reasons for this. Of course, there is the obvious biological-father angle mentioned earlier, which would probably be sufficient on its own. However, let's get to the important issues.

First of all, Andy Taylor raised Opie in his early childhood. He taught him all the basic lessons of life—he made Opie the lovable child that he was. Who taught him to fish, skip stones, and whistle catchy theme songs? Who taught him not to fight with the school bully? Who laughed alongside him when Barney locked himself in the jail cell? Who loved him even though he didn't get first place in the running race? Andy Taylor did! He was there. He was the best father ever, dammit!

And just because he's a single parent doesn't mean Opie wouldn't get the love and attention he deserves from a mother. Good ol' Aunt Bee is there to comfort him and to cook him nourishing meals. (You know she has to be a good cook just by looking at the size of her.) And, of course, Barney Fife is always there to lend a hand and useful advice when it's needed (or even if it's not).

The Cunninghams—well, let's just say they're a bit shady, and Solomon would see right through their ploy. Mr. C runs a hardware store. Have you ever met an honest hardware store manager? I didn't think so. What about that mysterious older brother who we never see? My guess is that he's locked in the basement somewhere. And then there's this motorcycle-riding hoodlum in black leather named "The Fonz" who's always hanging around their house. Not exactly a good influence on little Richie! Solomon will recognize that the Cunninghams are in fact horrible parents, and will deny them custody.

BRIAN: Zzzzzzzz—oh, I'm sorry. Are you finally done now? My goodness, I've seen manifestos that didn't run that long. No problem, it gave me some time to take a nap as well as practice my "In-A-Gadda-Da-Vida" drum solo. It also gave me some time to do some light reading: the Old Testament™. This match begins and ends with King Solomon, and the Old Testament (OT) is where he hangs out.

While some of your points *might* be relevant if the proceedings were being heard by some flaky *Divorce Court*–type judge, they will be useless on Solomon. Someone raised in the OT will have a whole different perspective on things. Remember, back then, if someone stole your oxen or your ass, you could stone them to death. *Legally!* And Solomon's parents only got together because Solomon's father, David, had Solomon's mother's (Bathsheba's) first husband (Uriah) killed! Thus, we must look at things from Solomon's warped, ultraviolent, *Pulp Fiction*-esque™ perspective. And there are three major factors to be concerned with here:

1. Birthright. They're ALWAYS talking about birthrights and such in the OT. Undoubtedly, the Cunninghams will also claim to be the biological parents of Richie. With no records to know for sure, this can only be a wash. And so what if Richie has an older brother no one's ever seen? Solomon will probably assume that Richie had him killed in order to inherit his birthright. That's something he can respect.

2. Impression. Solomon was the ruler of a kingdom for forty years. Is he going to be impressed by some guy with a badge from some small-time hick town? Of course not. What will he be impressed by? Mr. C's lodge connections. Lodges are the closest thing to royalty in American society today. Thus, a common bond will be formed between Mr. C and the king.

3. Age. How old is Richie in this scenario? Sixteen? Seventeen? When Solomon was that age he was ruler of all of Israel, had married seventy-five women and was wiping the blood of Benjamites off his scimitar. Is this guy going to be worried about which side will best "nurture" Richie in the best "environment"? No! He's going to be wondering why this guy doesn't already have three wives and eight kids working a plot of land. He would rather declare Richie an adult, but since that is not an option, he'll have to settle for the next best thing: leaving him with the Cunninghams. Why send him to the home that would smother him with love and treat him

like he's perpetually eight years old? You don't become a man that way. The Cunninghams win before you can say King Solomon's Mines™.

STEVE: Thanks for "The Gospel according to Brian." It's just as long and boring as those actual Gospel chapters in the Bible are. You've also managed to twist the Bible to suit your needs, just like Jimmy Bakker. All you need now is for people to start sending you their life savings and to have your wife start wearing ludicrous amounts of makeup.

You can't discount Andy Taylor. He is a master of legal knowledge. After all, he is Matlock. He always wins his cases. In fact, King Solomon will have a special weakness for him. As we all know, and as Grandpa Simpson has told us, old people hate everything, except for *Matlock*. Since five thousand years counts as old, even for Solomon, Solomon must also like *Matlock*, and thus award Opie to Andy "Matlock" Taylor. In addition, Andy and Barney will produce all manner of police reports (he is a sheriff, after all) showing that beyond a doubt Opie belongs to Andy and that the Cunninghams are evil Satan-worshipping child molesters with criminal records. Case closed.

You also can't forget about Barney. If by some chance the Cunninghams did win, Barney is just gung-ho enough to go after Richie/Opie and steal him back. Dare I say he might even take the bullet out of his pocket and actually place it into his gun? Barney Fife with a loaded gun is something to be avoided!

In the end, Opie will be fishing along the river again and eating heartily at Aunt Bee's table (after doing his homework, of course). Mr. Cunningham will resort back to selling Glad Sandwich Bags, and Mrs. C will run off and elope with the Fonz. A happy ending for all.

BRIAN: Boy, you just don't know when to shut up, do you? Suicide Prevention Hotline operators on Ritalin don't have an attention span long enough to listen to you ramble on.

And yes, I did say "ramble." You speak without ever stopping to check the validity of your statements. First off, the Gospels are anything BUT boring. You've got journeys, tyrants, criminals, mass slayings, prostitutes, mobs, executions, resurrections, and miracles aplenty. A real page turner! I couldn't put it down! Second, you claim I "twist the Bible" to suit my own needs, but then don't say what it is that I twist. It's all there for the whole (literate) world to see, Steve. Back up your claims! Third, this whole *Matlock* thing. Yes, it is true that old people love *Matlock*. Unfortunately, King Solomon is TOO old to love *Matlock*. When's the last time we ever heard Mr. Burns praise or even discuss *Matlock*? Never! If the oldest man in Springfield can ignore *Matlock*, surely the oldest judge in the Midwest can as well.

And for my final point I'd like to take you back to the OT once again. Who did Solomon have as his leaders, as his most trusted associates and advisors? Lawyers? I don't think so. Solomon probably doesn't even know what a lawyer is, so I don't see him taking too much stock in what Matlock has to say. No, the correct answer is priests! Solomon had several priests as his chief officials (check 1 Kings 4:1–6 for the record). And who is on the side of the Cunninghams? None other than Father Dowling himself! With all the mystery-solving prowess of Matlock (despite the lower ratings), he would surely be able to dig up as much dirt as anyone else (like that brothel of an apartment building Barney ran later in life). But the difference is that Solomon would listen to and believe Father Dowling, just as if he were Abiathar himself! Cunninghams in a rout.

Oh, and you were right about one thing, Steve. Barney Fife with a loaded gun is indeed something to be avoided. It's called *The Shakiest Gun in the West* and it sucked worse than *The Ghost and Mr. Chicken* and *The Love God?* combined.

THE OUTCOME

Andy Taylor (50.1%) edges out The Cunninghams (49.9%).

THE PEANUT GALLERY™

Okay, without wasting time explaining why the Cunninghams are the ultimate all-American Midwest-valued nuclear family (they are), let me instead address the shortcomings of Andy Taylor.

1. Not only is Andy Taylor a single parent, he's a police officer. Having little Opie around the police station is a recipe for disaster. It's only a question of time before Barney pulls that bullet out of his pocket, loads his gun, and accidentally blows Opie's face off. Any judge, particularly Solomon, should recognize such a dangerous environment. The only domestic risk the Cunninghams pose is the potential to catch the crabs from Pinky Tuscadero. Score one for the Cunninghams.

2. Remember *Salvage 1*? No one else does, either. Suffice to say that Andy has no compunction about throwing away his life savings and a profitable business in order to build a lame-themed weekly serial about a man and his rocket. NASA may be privatizing, but I don't think they'll be calling Andy with any fat contracts. Financial irresponsibility won't look good in court. Mr. C: 2, Andy: 0.

Besides, have you ever noticed Andy is NEVER MARRIED in ANY of these shows? I'm not so sure he IS the biological father, if you know what I mean.

—*Bill Lindich*

I realize that Matlock never technically lost a case. But there's a fault in that logic. Matlock once got a guilty woman off. The reason: He's a dirty old man. This kind of thing will come back to haunt him, as will his recent album of gospel songs.

—Matt Lynch

As a good lawyer, Matlock will do research on the Cunningham "Family" and he will notice an astonishing fact: The "older brother" of Richie Cunningham appeared on only three episodes of the show. Admittedly, this ain't the most shocking fact in the world. What is disturbing, however, is that he was played by three different actors!

King Solomon just doesn't have any way to look at this but one: The Cunninghams have been stealing adolescent boys from their rightful homes for years! Richie is the fourth such victim THAT WE KNOW OF! And notice, these "sons" all keep disappearing. . . . It was only a matter of time before Richie "joined the Navy and went overseas for a while. . . ."

Luckily, Solomon is a firm believer in the Code of Hammurabi, so he would be able to devise a just punishment for the Cunninghams: to be kidnapped and raised by Wilford Brimley and the rest of the *Our House* family, doomed to a lifetime of Quaker Oatmeal and bad geriatric movies.

—Cornboy

The most important thing we must remember is that Howard Cunningham, a devout Republican, was unable to convince his son to vote for Dwight Eisenhower. This shows a lack of control over the boy, and being from the old school of parenting, Solomon would have to go with Andy, who would never raise a son to vote for Adlai Stevenson.

—Brendan W. Guy

[After much deliberation] they decide to let Richie Opie Taylor Cunningham (ROTC) decide for himself. They give him twenty-four hours.

That night he dreams. He is playing saxophone with his buddies.

"Put your head on my shoouuuuuullllllderrrrrrr . . ."

"I still got it."

"Yep, yep, yep, yep, yep, yep, yep, yep."

"Ayyyyyyyy."

"Schlemiel, schlemazel, Hossenpfeffer Incorporated."

"Joanie, you're grounded!"

In his sleep, Richie smiles. But then, his dream turns ugly. He is living in a black and white world. . . .

"Oooh, the boy needs a haircut."

"Well, gooooolllllllllllleeeeeeee."

"Emmett, I want that vehicle outa here!"

"Now, Barney, just settle down."

"Andeeeeeeee! Andeeee! Dinner's on the table!"

"But, paw!"

"Oooh, the boy needs a haircut!" (*snip snip*)

He awakes screaming. Mrs. C comes in and gives him some hot chocolate to comfort him. And Richie Cunningham realizes you can never go back to Mayberry.

—*The Listmeister*

James Bond vs. Indiana Jones

THE SETTING

"The Nazis are at it again. This time they're combing Jerusalem in search of the Egg of Turin, a Fabergé egg made by John the Baptist. We need you to go in and get it before they do."

"The Egg of Turin? Isn't that kind of a silly artifact to chase after?"

"Well, dammit, Indy, that's what you get for finding all the good ones! And, besides, it isn't totally silly. This Egg is not only cholesterol-free, but it gives its owner the power to also be cholesterol-free, and, thus, to live forever. This is a power Hitler cannot have."

"I'll take the first red line to Jerusalem."

"Oh, and, Indy. The Nazis have joined forces with someone else, someone also bent on world domination. That's gotten the Brits involved. This Egg is too powerful, Indy, for even our allies to get ahold of."

Superfriends *narrator voice:* "Meanwhile, thousands of miles away in London, England . . . "

"Blofeld's at it again, Double-O Seven. He's teamed up with the Nazis in search of another one of those blasted eggs. If they get a hold of it, it could mean the end of the free world. Talk to Q and get what you need. Miss Moneypenny will give you the password for your contact in Syria right after she flirts with you. Oh, and the Americans are sending in one of their best men. This is a power that Her Majesty's government, and hers alone, must have, is that clear? Don't blunder your mission this time, Double-O Seven."

So, Steve, which hero tracks down the Biblical Super Egg first?

Please note: This match involves Sean Connery as James Bond. Any suggestion that any of those other Bond-wannabes should be involved will result in a severe flogging.

THE COMMENTARY

STEVE: I gotta go with Bond on this one. First of all, Bond has his gadgets. Q branch comes through with the goodies that always seem to help 007 at the most appropriate moments. They always catch the bad guys by surprise and save the day. All Indy has is his whip and revolver. The Nazis are wise to this from two previous movies and will be ready and waiting for him. Such trifling weapons are, of course, insignificant to Blofeld, who regularly works with much more sophisticated weapons like poison gases and high-powered lasers. Meanwhile, Bond will easily grab the Egg by killing the guards with his explosive cigarettes, and then deftly escape in his mini-hovercraft.

Another important factor is, of course, that Sean Connery (aka James Bond) is also Indy's father. With Jones Sr.'s superior archaeology experience and biblical knowledge combined with the James Bond class, there is no chance that Indy will escape with the Egg. And if somehow Indy does get his hands on the Egg, Belloq is likely to come and snatch it away from him anyhow.

No one can top James Bond in the "class" contest. Bond will obtain the Egg after a typical classy evening: He will begin with some cocktails, and then play some baccarat (dressed in a tux, of course), which will win him the notice of a buxom young woman with a slutty name. They'll go back to his hotel room, and after a couple hours of passion, he'll awake in the Nazi/Blofeld secret base (sleeping drug in the cocktail!). He'll escape the death trap set by the Nazis and then recover the Egg as described above. Bond has obtained the Egg after an evening of partying in the traditional Bond style. No real work, just class and savvy. Indy has none of this—he's all guts-and-glory wannabe. He'll try to shoot and sneak his way into wherever the Nazis are hiding the Egg, and in the process get the crap beat out of him, as always. He'll likely spend the rest of his life a Nazi prisoner, unless he is fortunate enough to be imprisoned at Stalag 13.

BRIAN: Bond has no shot here, Steve. First of all, with any kind of halfway decent competition, Bond won't be able to get the job done fast enough because he will be too busy A) having sex; B) recovering from the bad position having sex put him in, and/or C) burying the woman he just had sex with. But even more importantly, you have the Nazis involved. And if they're involved, then they're in charge, not Blofeld. That means three things: 1) The villains will be drinking beer, not wine. Without being able to expose hit men or evildoers by their ignorance of vino, Bond won't know who his enemies really are. 2) When Nazis capture bad guys, they usually kill them straight out. They don't devise some ultra-complex and ironic way of killing their prisoners. And they *definitely* don't decide to divulge their evil plans right before they knock somebody off. With no chance to escape (we all know he's going to be caught sometime), and with no chance to figure out the evil plan, Bond himself will have no chance.

3) Reality. That's right: With the Nazis involved, that means this is the real world, not the Bond-world. Bond must now obey the Laws of Physics™, something he hasn't ever had to do before. Suddenly, jumping on that helicopter from the smoking, pilotless plane won't be quite so easy. And he also won't have infinitely sized pockets. I once saw him fortuitously find a safe and then pull a safecracking device out of his coat! What does he have under there, a Bat Utility Belt™? Not here, he won't. Without his gadgets and usual M.O.'s, Bond is helpless.

Which leaves Indy. If he's anything but an idiot, he'll win this. And I think his résumé speaks for itself: extensive experience in recovering Biblical artifacts, previous battles with Nazis and several types of hostile natives, excellent with a whip. Indy finds the Egg, loses the Egg, then regains the Egg when the Wrath of God™ wipes out another Mediterranean island. (Oh, and if you can use the fact that Bond is actually Indy's father, then I can point out how Indy has Luke, The Force, Leia in a Gold Bikini, etc. Let's not go there.)

STEVE: Your arguments are so riddled with errors that I don't even know where to start. First of all, the Nazis are worse than *Batman* villains for leaving the hero for dead after telling them the whole evil plot. Didn't they seal Indy in the the Well of Souls™ to die amid the poisonous asps? Didn't they tie Indy up to witness the opening of the Ark? Didn't they tie him up with his father in the German castle for "future execution"? I won't even get started with other sources such as *Hogan's Heroes* or *Force 10 from Navarone* (with Harrison Ford, no less).

If James Bond is guilty of violating the Laws of Physics™, then Indy has to be locked away for life for all his violations. Sure, Bond twists things now and then, but Indy is doing it all the time. Let's see—jumping out of an airplane and having a rubber raft break your fall, having a runaway mining cart jump from one track to the next, and of course the famous "dragged under the moving truck, holding on with a whip, all while bleeding from a gunshot wound in the shoulder." Gimme a break!

Your last paragraph makes me laugh. How many biblical artifacts has he actually recovered? Zero! The government (urged on by a Vatican conspiracy, probably) stole the Ark away from him. And of course he couldn't remove the Holy Grail without destroying all those neat traps that took millions of special-effects dollars to create. Indy actually has nothing to his credit at all. Bond, on the other hand, always goes the distance. He always stops the nuclear bomb from going off (at least three times, if I'm not mistaken); recovers the encryption device; and defeats Blofeld and his evil plans, and usually a whole gang of thugs and maybe even the Russians. Compared to this, recovering an Egg from the Nazis is simplicity itself.

BRIAN: Aha! If recovering the Egg from the Nazis was the goal, Bond would have a chance. But the real goal is to *find* the Egg before the Nazis do. And that is where Indy's archaeological expertise will blow Bond away.

And I, in turn, laugh at your middle paragraph. The idea that Indy defies the Laws of Physics™ worse than Bond! First of all, most of the examples you give are from *The Temple of Doom*, which is not only the armpit of the trilogy but is also noticeably Nazi-free. With made-up baddies and mystic forces, physics could be suspended. So all that leaves you with is your unsubstantiated ridicule of one of the finest stunts in cinematic history. Seems to me there really was someone under that truck; it wasn't creative editing. And remember how beat up Indy was afterwards? That's *real*, Steve. Now, if Bond had tried something like that in one of his movies, he would have easily performed the maneuver, dusted off his wrinkle-free Armani, proceeded to boink the woman driver who had just tried to kill him, and *then* stopped the truck. If he tries that in this realistic scenario, he'll end up like so much limey roadkill.

And don't even get me started on your analysis of the participants' résumés! All Bond has ever done is out-thunk a few villains with the collective IQ of *one Scooby-Doo* villain. Indy, however, *has* retrieved artifacts. He did recover the Ark, after all. Sure, it's not in his den, but at least Hitler didn't get ahold of it. And maybe the Grail isn't in his cupboard, but I didn't see anyone else smart enough to find it (and that includes John Cleese). After Indy finds the Egg and brings it back to the States, it is deemed too dangerous for all involved. It's placed in an unmarked egg carton and buried deep inside a huge Winn Dixie warehouse outside Hoboken.

THE OUTCOME

Indiana Jones (63%) buries James Bond (37%).

THE PEANUT GALLERY™

Knowing his enemy's weaknesses for women and drinking, Indy, after a long, expensive, choreographed bar-fight scene, would have enlisted the help of Marion. Bond and Marion engage in a long, evenly matched drinking challenge until he collapses from kidney failure and the pain of living with over fifty known sexually transmitted diseases. Indy gets the Egg, and Bond lives the rest of his life bedridden on dialysis, every day boinking a new nurse.

—Al

Despite all of Bond's gadgets, nothing can compare to Indy's magic fedora. Oft forgotten, this hat has powers beyond those of mortal Q. Regardless of the predicament, it will always return. Indy need only strap the Egg in as soon as he finds it, and fly home. When he arrives, through the magic of Fedora Express, the Egg will be there waiting for him.

—Micah Johnson (Indiana Jones WWW Page,
http://www.softaid.net/msjohnso/)

Despite their incredible skills, mental ability, charisma, internal fortitude, and unbelievable luck, it is clear that both Mr. Bond and Mr. Jones should be long dead by now. Time and time again, they escape the hopeless trap and achieve the absurd with nothing more than what can be described as Divine Intervention™. Yes, God is the only explanation for their fantastic success. So clearly, the new owner of immortality will be the one that can best use it for the betterment of mankind. The candidates:

1. The Nazis—NO! Anyone stupid enough to fight a war on two fronts AND attack Russia in winter AND trust on Italy as a

valued military ally has no chance. Blofeld would probably put them out of their misery himself by sending them to find the Beer Keg of Turin in the middle of the Arabian desert and then ironically wipe them out with nerve gas.

2. Blofeld—No! Any man who is willing to expose billions to World War III and nuclear winter for millions in gold that would be utterly useless in a postapocalyptic world is too evil and too clueless for immortality. In addition, if he ruled the world, everyone would have to own cats and God would have to deal with the smell and all the kitty litter for all of eternity. After Bond shoots him dead, God *ZOTS* him a couple of times to make sure.

3. James Bond—No. Agent 007 has sex with almost every beautiful woman he comes into contact with. True, this does lead to more people screaming "OH GOD!" to the heavens, but consider the consequences. With immortality, he has the time to mate with EVERY female. Within generations, every human will have Bond as an ancestor, leading to redneck-level inbreeding. Just consider billions of Forrest Gumps wearing red-with-pink-polka-dot tuxedos playing high-stakes games of Old Maid, drinking Budweiser Martinis and bedding down the Fabulous Moolah in a roadside motel in Monaco. EEK! Bond is conveniently trapped in a cave-in with three female companions to work out his version of the "Middle East Peace Process."

4. Indiana Jones—Yes! The only person left, he is too smart to let the Egg fall into the wrong hands and too humble to use it for world domination. And I'm sure God would appreciate the irony of the Nazis, a Nazi wannabe, and a WASP playboy being defeated by a couple of Jews—Steven Spielberg and Harrison Ford (one-quarter Jewish).

—*Paul Golba*

The Brady Bunch vs. The Partridge Family

THE SETTING

(Backa-wacka wow, wakka wakka, backa-wacka wow)

"Hi, this is Bob, along with my esteemed colleague Bob, LIVE from the Forum in Los Angeles, California, for the third and deciding game in the battle for The President's Cup, the highest prize in Roller Derby! So, Bob, what do you make of tonight's match-up?"

"Well, Bob, it doesn't get any better than this. Tonight's battle will be a test of endurance, speed, experience, strength, and brute force. And no one in the country has better combinations of those than our two teams meeting here tonight. I just spoke with Reuben, the Partridge coach, and he says his troops are pumped and ready to go. I haven't been able to talk to Sam, however, as he closed his locker room to the press after that incident last week, but we all know that the Bradys will be fired up. The crowd's going wild; it's gonna be a great one, Bob."

"Thank you for those superficial and noncommittal comments, Bob. I'd like to add that things could get interesting with a tough draw at referee. Tom Arnold and Roseanne will really stay on top of things tonight. So let's take it down to rinkside and to Steve and Brian for their in-depth analysis and predictions!"

THE COMMENTARY

STEVE: Well, Brian, this match-up was a long time in coming, but it's worth it. And I'm glad it's not one of those sissy talent show competitions that the Brady Bunch always seem to be entering. Of course, we all know that the Partridges have musical talent while the Bradys have none. This scenario, however, promises to be a Roller Derby match for the ages.

Brian, I just came from the locker room after an interview with Coach Sam "The Butcher" Franklin. And I have to say that the underdog Partridges could really pull off an upset victory if they play up to their potential today. The Bradys, who are playing with some absences, are unusually weak. According to Sam, two of the team's superstars are unable to play today. The team captain, Mike Brady, had to leave at the last minute to find his lost architect plans somewhere on a roller coaster in Ohio. And the aggressive Cindy Brady is unavailable due to being at a threesome photo session which she couldn't reschedule. This leaves both Laurie and Danny Partridge with openings in a vulnerable Brady defense, which could allow them to score.

The Partridges are looking pumped up and ready to play today. Danny's boxing career has him ready for this match today. Keith's all fired up, and . . . Wait! What's this? Shirley Partridge has rummaged through Mrs. Brady's duffel bag and found a bottle of Wesson oil! Shirley is covering herself in its slippery cholesterol-free goodness! She'll be so slick that they won't be able to stop her! The presence of oil (and thus fat) has drawn the attention of Roseanne, who's telling Shirley she must remove the oil. Shirley has flipped her off and is now lacing up her skates. Roseanne is trying to eject Shirley, but Shirley has no intention of going anywhere. This match is heating up before it's begun!

BRIAN: No question those two absences will hurt the Bradys, Steve, but there are two more absences which will help them. MRIs confirmed this week that the injury Tracy suffered in the semis against the Ingallses was, in fact, a torn ACL, and she's gone for the season. Plus, Jan still hasn't recovered from a traumatic baby-sitting experience several months ago. The match-up of Carol, Marcia, and the three boys against Shirley, Keith, Danny, Chris, and Laurie heavily favors the Bradys!

But aside from that, I just don't think the Partridges have come to play tonight. First off, you've got Laurie with her face in those legal briefings instead of studying game strategies. Then, you've got Shirley skating around tentatively in that "Caution! Nervous Mother Skating" T-shirt. Not exactly something to instill confidence on the team. And now she's covered in cooking oil. This shows a lack of experience on her part, Steve. She might slip through the defense, if she ever got to the defense; if her kids can't grab ahold of her arm to sling her forward, she's got no chance.

Plus, talking with Danny and Keith just a few moments ago, I got the feeling that a whole lotta lovin' is what they'll be bringin' into the rink tonight. Well, unfortunately for them, the Bradys will be bringin' elbows. And I don't think beating up on Donny Osmond is going to help Danny against Greg, the Brady Enforcer. It's clear to me that the Bradys are into this more than the Partridges, and that will just be amplified by the pro-Brady crowd here tonight. Not too surprising, though, considering the Brady resurgence the past few years with their movies while the Partridge Family is lucky to get reruns on Nick at Nite. This town loves the Bradys! [*Crowd begins to cheer.*] Hey, Los Angeles! Who do you love?! [*"The Bradys!!"*] Who's number one? [*"The Bradys!!"*] Who's gonn—

STEVE: Folks! A terrible accident has just occurred! It seems that somehow a folding chair struck Brian in the back of the head and flipped him over the railing. Just like in *Star Trek*! A few fans threw him back into the rink, and it appears that the skaters are mostly managing to avoid running him over during their warmup laps. While he's coming to, I want to talk with Reuben Kincaid, manager of the Partridge Family team. So Reuben, I understand you have a secret weapon which will defeat the Brady family tonight?

Reuben: Yes, Steve, tonight the Brady family is certain to lose. At great expense I have had the infamous Cursed Tiki™ brought back from its sacred resting place in Hawaii, and have secretly planted it among the Bradys' belongings in a place where they will never find it. Its bad luck will insure their downfall. Just moments ago, a tarantula was spotted crawling out of Alice's duffel bag.

STEVE: It sounds like you have this victory all but wrapped up. With the powers of darkness working for you, it doesn't seem like you could lose. Ahh, I see Brian has collected himself. Brian, are you all right? Oh my! You've torn your network jacket! That'll be coming out of your pay, mister.

BRIAN: What?! Who are you?! Why's that woman so shiny? Whoa! Steve? Hi, I'm back now. Boy, that was a stroke of bad luck there. Wonder how that happened.

Reuben: Maybe it's that Cursed Tiki. Maybe it's bad luck for everybody. Oh, no! What have I done— AAUUGH!!

BRIAN: Ewww!! Well, that's what he gets for not wearing a helmet. Anyway, this apparent voodoo curse definitely favors the Bradys, Steve. With voodoo comes freak injuries, and that's when depth becomes important. The Bradys have Alice available if one of the starters gets injured, and there's always the chance that Mike could make it back by halftime. The Partridges have no subs: Snake's in Africa doling out food to Sally Struthers's kids, and I don't think *Mister* Partridge will be showing up anytime soon. We're a couple of loose railings and hard elbows away from a Partridge forfeit.

And, again, it all comes down to attitude. "C'mon get happy"? I'd even wager to say that the Partridges are here mainly to get some publicity for their upcoming Uruguayan tour rather then to actually win this match. Well, if they sing for any more than five seconds, expect Roseanne to grab her crotch, spit, and then beat them silly with the Gatorade cooler. In contrast, the Bradys are just plain mean. Six kids and one bathroom will do that to a family. And if Sam has brought along any of his meat-chopping devices . . . well, let's just say it could be worse than *Rollerball*. I see the Bradys clinching it by half-time. For Steve, I'm Batman; now back to Bob and Bob for the play-by-play.

THE OUTCOME

The Brady Bunch (66%) rolls over the
Partridge Family (34%).

THE PEANUT GALLERY™

While the Bradys are washing off their Wesson and picking up their teeth with the hopes that they can be reimplanted, the Partridges play a rousing concert, with a new song: "Hey, I think I kicked ass."

—*Sluggo at UIC*

Shirley, lubed-up Partridge matriarch, sends a greased elbow straight into Carol's temple. Little does she know Carol and Mike have been lighting up in Greg's Happenin' Attic Pad™ and with one flick of a Bic on her oiled-up body a roast Partridge goes flailing into the middle of the track, colliding with the Connors and starting a grease fire of biblical proportions. All eyes turn to Keith and Greg. Greg, busy hitting on groovy chick™ Laurie, gets hammered to the floor. Enraged, he gets up and tears off his uniform, revealing . . . Johnny Bravo! Calling forth such Mentos-level coolness™ seals victory for the Bradys and a year's supply of tarantula repellant.

—*Steve L.*

The factors which will lead the Brady Bashers to victory are as obvious as the broken nose on Marcia's face:

1. Teamwork: Remember the architectural-plans-in-the-tube relay in the amusement park? Speed, coordination, pushing themselves beyond the reasonable limits of teenage endurance:

This is the stuff of victory.

2. The "Honey" factor: Who has the greater number of babes on their team? Who wouldn't like to be run over by Marcia and Carol, not to mention what Cindy is capable of doing to a man? The male contingent of the Partridge team will be reduced to drooling, hormone-hamstrung roadkill.

—*Marcia's Slave (prizm1@erols.com)*

The first time Shirley Partridge goes down, she stays down, too slippery with Wesson to regain her footing. Danny is easily handled by Carol Brady; he has a history of losing scuffles with anybody in women's clothing. Laurie starts complaining about all the fouling, but this is no place for a rulebook lawyer. Over the rail she goes. No appeal. By this time, Alice has begun handing out various kitchen implements to passing teammates, and the thrashing that ensues is terrible, though mercifully brief. Now for a rousing chorus of "I Woke Up in Traction This Morning"!

—*Call me Shane*

How did both families reach the arena? The Bradys had to drive that piece of $#!+ green station wagon that Greg couldn't even stop in time to avoid that egg (the memory of his failure will surely weaken the Bradys' key player [further]). Traveling by station wagon is tiring and cramped. The Partridges, on the other hand, will be cruising in style in that bad-ass™ Love Bus™ of theirs. In addition to traveling in comfort, the Partridge Family is used to road trips; the Bradys are used to sitting at home, fanning their asses on that AstroTurf lawn of theirs.

—*Tiger*

Pinky & The Brain vs. Dogbert

THE SETTING

As night falls on an unnamed industrial park, two inhabitants of Acme Labs™ awaken and begin to go about their business. Brain tinkers in the lab while Pinky mindlessly sits in front of the TV.

"Hey, Brain, this television news show here just said that ninety percent of the world's computers use Microsoft products! Narf!"

Brain's ears perk up and an evil grin appears across his face: "Pinky, are you pondering what I am pondering?"

"I think so, Brain, but hasn't the world had enough of Tony Danza in a situation comedy?"

Brain slaps Pinky and explains: "If we could take over Microsoft, then we could control ninety percent of the world's computers, and thus, THE WORLD!" Brain hurries off to work out the details of tonight's project.

Unbeknownst to Brain, another attempt is being made at taking over Microsoft, and thus the world. However, this attempt comes from within Microsoft itself. Enter Dogbert, management consultant. Dogbert, who has finally decided the world is worthy of him as a ruler, has spent all night drawing up new org charts, project flowcharts, and management policies. With these new materials, and the current nonexistent management skills of Microsoft, the takeover of the world is at hand!

So Brian, which of these cartoon characters bent on world domination will succeed?

THE COMMENTARY

BRIAN: Dogbert is so far out of Brain's league that I almost feel sorry for the little mongrel. He's really just a novice at world domination, tinkering a bit here and there when he feels like it. And while he's had some successes, he usually gets bored or distracted and never finishes the job. He just doesn't have what it takes, and that's why he's never made it to the next level.

Brain, however, is *obsessed* with taking over the world. He tries to do it "every night." And despite Dogbert's repeated failures, Brain *has* taken over the world many times. Remember when he built Chia Earth™? He ruled the old Earth for quite a while before it was destroyed by a comet. And after the production and release of *Brain's Song*, he temporarily grasped control of the world, right before becoming a laughingstock. True, he never keeps control of the world, but that isn't the point here, is it? He will take over Microsoft and then rule the world for sixty seconds until he loses everything when the mother of Bill Gates's love child sues the company for eighty billion in child support and wins.

And let us not forget about Brain's incredible powers and abilities. He's appeared in biblical times, medieval England, the future, and several times and places in between. He constructed the aforementioned life-size papier-mâché replica of Earth. He bested Little John with the buck-and-a-quarter quarterstaff and Robin Hood at archery. With these kinds of abilities and traveling powers, no task is too Herculean for Brain and his adequate cohort, Pinky. What resources does Dogbert have? Ratbert? Dogbert gives up and starts licking himself as Brain seizes control of Microsoft's board of directors.

STEVE: The reason Dogbert hasn't, as you say, "made it to the next level" is because he simply hasn't put his mind to it yet. The world simply wasn't worthy of his domination. Now that this fact has changed, there's no stopping him. And Brain's obsession with world domination is his downfall. History has shown us time and again that those obsessed with world domination always fail. Examples include Lex Luthor, Khan, and Ernst Blofeld. They have repeatedly lost, primarily due to the blinding influences of their obsession. If they could take a step back and look at things with broader perspective, they usually could have averted their downfall. Brain will be like a horse with blinders on, and won't be ready for Dogbert's competition, leading to his predictable loss. In fact, has Brain ever experienced any competition? I don't think he can stand up to it. That's why he always hangs out with Pinky.

Of course, the painfully obvious reason why Dogbert must win is that Brain always screws things up in the end. The example you cite in which Brain takes over the world for sixty seconds is meaningless and counts for diddly-squat. For effectual control, it must remain indefinitely. Of course, Brain is somehow always denied control of the world, or has it taken away at the last minute. It's as predictable as Gilligan not getting off his island, or as Wile E. Coyote not catching the Road Runner. Dogbert has no such curse to hinder his plans. As a matter of fact, he always seems to achieve what he sets out to do, no matter how ludicrous. He hasn't put his mind to it yet, but when he does, it will be painfully simple for him to exercise complete control over the mindless drones in Microsoft.

BRIAN: I didn't realize that you'd started drinking in the mornings again, Steve. Regardless, where in the scenario is anything said about "effectual control" of the world? The race here is to take over Microsoft and thus the world; there are no restrictions on how long one must rule the world. And, as discussed, Brain has conquered the world several times already.

And then you try to tell us that Lex Luthor, Khan, and Ernst Blofeld failed due to the "blinding influences of their obsession"??!! No, Steve, they failed because they went up against Superman, the Federation, and James Bond! Brain has no such annoying all-powerful do-gooder counterpart, and thus will not suffer the same fate as these other classic villains. And to say that the reason Dogbert has not made it to that next level is because he never really wanted to is an awfully *convenient* argument, Steve. Yeah, and Michael Jordan never made it to the majors because he didn't want to play in a dome.

And considering this is a race, time is of the essence. Brain has his own show. Thus, he will be able to use 80 percent of his time to do his work, the other 20 percent going toward commercials and those grating prepubescent WB! hosts. Dogbert, however, is but a small player in the Dilbert universe. Dilbert and Dilbert-related story lines will dominate 90 percent of the time for Dogbert, if he's even allowed to appear.

Thus, left with a meager 10 percent, Dogbert will barely have a chance to compile a plan before Brain has conquered and already lost control of the world. Twice.

STEVE: If you seriously believe that Brain has "conquered the world several times already," then I suppose you also believe that Gilligan has escaped his island several times too. Sure, they got on the raft and headed out to sea, but it sank just as they were leaving the lagoon. Sure, technically they left the island for a few moments, but in effect, they might as well not have bothered. In my book it doesn't count, plain and simple.

Your points about speed are correct (except for your exaggerated 10 percent), but you've left out a few important facts that drastically alter their relative speeds. First, the majority of Brain's experience in days past entailed only a small portion of a larger show (*Animaniacs*) in which to do his work, just as with Dogbert now. And like Dogbert, sometimes he didn't even appear at all. Sure, he has his own show now, but so now does Dogbert have his own outlet: Dogbert's New Ruling Class*. Thus that argument is a wash. Second, we see Brain almost entirely in reruns. He isn't often seen doing anything new these days. And even when he is doing something new, it's only on a weekly basis, not daily. Dogbert is as fresh as today's newspaper, possibly even fresher since he motors along on the Internet as well. The result: Dogbert takes over Microsoft, then The World™, and as ruler, has Acme Labs™ bulldozed to the ground.

THE OUTCOME

Dogbert (51%) rules over Pinky & The Brain (49%).

---

*DNRC is an Internet club of people who associate with Dogbert and will become the new leaders of the world after Dogbert takes over.

THE PEANUT GALLERY™

"Gee, Brain, what are we going to do tonight?"

"The same thing we do every night, Pinky. Try to take over the world!"

"Eureka! I have calculated the 'Take Over the World Formula'™ on the computer! Now all we need to do is print it so we can create the formula!"

Suddenly, a Windows 95 dialogue box appears on Brain's computer as he clicks on "Print":

THIS PROGRAM HAS PERFORMED AN ILLEGAL OPERATION AND WILL BE SHUT DOWN. IF PROBLEM PERSISTS, CONTACT YOUR VENDOR.

"NO!!!!" The formula is lost forever.

(*Meanwhile . . .*)

"Yes! I've accessed Microsoft's computer system! Now to make one little change."

CEO: WILLIAM H. GATES III

Dogbert clicks on it.

CEO: DOGBERT

Dogbert clicks "OK," and a dialogue box appears:

THERE IS NOT ENOUGH MEMORY TO PERFORM THIS TASK.

"NO!!!!!"

Another victory for the corporate giant known as Microsoft!

—*Nathan of Borg*

Fools! It's too late! Can't you tell? Those glasses! The computer savvy! The nonchalant disregard for going through conventional channels! Dogbert *IS* Bill Gates!

Dilbert: I was going through your room and I found this wig.

Dogbert: So. My secret is out. I was saving millions in taxes by legally declaring myself a dog. No matter. Plan B.

Dilbert: What are you doing with my birth certificate?

Dogbert: As per our agreement, we have now swapped identities, for tax purposes only. By the way, you owe $234,345,895 in back taxes.

Dilbert: Agreement? What agreement!?!

Dogbert: You must really read the license agreement on your software before opening it.

A no-Brainer.

—John Hunter

True Brain will conquer the world, but then he will hire Dogbert as a proactive consultant to monitor any action committees about revamping the world's mission statement. In effect, Dogbert wins, as he has the TRUE power over the world.

Pinky? He goes into marketing.

—Budo

It looks like a Dogbert victory to me, Bob. Initial advantage is Dogbert's, as when P&B first try to infiltrate, they discover the HR director is none other than the evil Catbert, and have to spend a few hours in a convenient hole in the wall, avoiding the cartoon cat in traditional cartoon mouse fashion.

In the meantime, Dogbert is finding that BG is even easier to dominate than the Pointy-Haired Boss™, and quickly takes over the Microsoft control center. However, even Saint Dogbert has trouble exorcising the Demons of Stupidity that constitute its Win95 OS. Luckily for him, P&B are sidetracked on the way there by Pinky realizing he's gay (big surprise there, folks) and having a torrid affair with Ratbert, while

Brain gets sidetracked admiring Dilbert's software. He makes a quick attempt at world domination using Dilbert's "Take Over the World" software beta, but is stopped by bugs and the firewall . . .

In the meantime, Dogbert has exorcised Win95, only to discover that the world has already been taken over by the Garbage Man, who did it twenty-five years ago as a grade-school prank. Since he likes Dogbert, he hands over the reins of power. Db is seen collecting garbage the next day, while the Garbage Man moves to Tahiti.

—martinl

Brain simply wants to rule the world. Nice, but hardly ambitious. Dogbert wants to enslave the human race, which is much more devious.

Dogbert would erode Microsoft's internal structure by creating a reverse org chart that would put Bill Gates at the bottom and tech support intake workers at the top. Thus "empowered," the Microserfs would contribute to the corporate chaos. Dogbert would set up Dilbert as a dummy CEO. Dilbert would have all the money and attention he could want, and could care less if Dogbert enslaved the human race.

—Capt. Rage™ Forder

Pinky & The Brain by a mile! The reason, this is the first believable plot that they've ever had! I'd have to say that taking over Microsoft is much easier than building a giant clothes dryer and zapping everyone with static cling.

—Chris Csont

Dogbert is very experienced at making screwy corporate logic work to his own advantage. While Brain is getting blank stares, Dogbert is convincing the board of MS to make him CEO because he has great hair.

—*Lord High Commander of Paper Clips, DNRC*

There's the great tradition of evil geniuses and/or criminal organizations bent on world domination named after body parts (The Claw, The Hand, The Foot, etc.). Here, we have not one, but two such individuals working in unison. I don't have a Dogbert on my body, and I'm reasonably sure that most others don't either (unless an overzealous fan got him tattooed there).

—*Blimpy the Lactose Intolerant Cat*

Dogbert has seen the corporate world from the inside and knows how to manipulate the cube-dwellers; he can twist the system to work to his advantage, while Pinky & The Brain would have to instigate a violent overthrow of the current system, setting up a new one in its place. Yes, they've proven time and again that they can do the violent overthrow bit, but they're not up to the task of governing. Dogbert has been training for it for years—DECADES, in dog time. We'll be seeing Dogbert courtside at Sonics games by round two of the playoffs.

—*Lionel Hutz*

Rocky vs. Rambo

THE SETTING

The crowd goes silent as the lights dim in anticipation of the featured match of the evening. The previous bouts have all been disappointments. Somehow, the heavily promoted fights of Hulk Hogan vs. Emo Phillips and Randy "Macho Man" Savage vs. Macaulay Culkin didn't last for the regulation fifteen rounds. Those who spent $150 for tonight's ringside seats are ready for some real action. The laser light show starts up along with the fog machines and deep rumbling bass undertones piped though the stadium's P.A. system.

"Ladies and gentlemen, your attention please. Tonight, in

The Ultimate World Fighting Championship CLXVIII, we bring you a duel for the crown of Ultimate Fighting!"

"In this corner, at five feet seven inches, 195 pounds, we have the ex–heavyweight champion of the world, the Italian Stallion, ROCKY BALBOA!"

Rocky's trainer, Mickey, pulls off Rocky's robe. The crowd, especially those from Philly, go wild.

"And in this corner, at five feet seven inches, 195 pounds, we have ex–Green Beret, Vietnam vet, winner of the Congressional Medal of Honor, John RAMBO!"

Colonel Trautman removes Rambo's camo outfit and takes away his knife. Rambo steps into the ring with an intense stare, ready for anything.

"Remember, any fighting style is allowed in the ring, but no weapons, please. Fighters to your corners . . . Let the fight begin!"

So, Brian, will the Boxer or the Beret be the best in this battle?

THE COMMENTARY

BRIAN: Rambo's completely out of his element here, Steve. Is this a mountainside in the Pacific Northwest? Or the jungles of Southeast Asia? No, it's the octagoned circle of Ultimate Fighting, far too exposed and restrictive for Rambo. What do you have when you strip Rambo of his weapons and stick him in a ring? You've got that guy from *Stop! or My Mom Will Shoot!* What do you have when you strip Rocky of any weapons and stick him in a ring? You've still got Rocky.

Rambo's true strengths come from the element of surprise and the use of weaponry; both of these factors have been neutralized. Rocky's true strengths come from the Eye of the Tiger™ and the Burning Heart™, and, not only are those still available, but they're just about to burst. Additionally, Rocky has proven his Grudge Match worth by defeating past champion and unofficial Grudge Match spokesperson Mr. T. Who has Rambo bested? A cocoon-loving alien and a two-bit Beverly Hills hood. Hardly impressive.

Poor Rambo will be facedown on the mat in seconds. Trautman's pleas to the referee to end the fight fall on deaf ears. As Rocky goes in for the kill, he realizes that snapping Rambo's neck won't erase the regrets of the past: Apollo won't be any less dead, and *Tango & Cash* won't be any less made. He refuses to proceed, and Judge Dredd rules in favor of Rocky by TKO. The crowd, disgusted by the brevity of the fight and this misplaced display of compassion, is left wishing that they had instead gone to see the more competitive Tank Abbott/Pete Becker rematch.

STEVE: Rambo is completely out of his element? Rambo's training is to *adapt* to his situation! He learned all of his guerrilla knowledge in Vietnam. When he ended up being put down by the man in Oregon, he easily adapted to the forests of the Pacific Northwest. He will just as easily adapt to the Ultimate Fighting arena. And we've already seen that Rambo doesn't need any weapons to win a fight, nor does the closed-in space of a ring hamper him. He escaped from a small prison cell, surrounded by four armed officers, using nothing but his bare hands and fighting skills. And he made it look easy.

Rambo's strength is that he can adapt. Rocky is a one-trick kind of guy. All he knows is boxing. When he's up against a nonboxer, he's in trouble. Just look at how Hulk Hogan toyed with him in *Rocky III*. Rambo will use his karate/kung fu/barroom fighting style (where just about anything goes) and will leave Rocky bewildered and not knowing what's coming next.

After a few broken arms and ribs, Rocky will fall unconscious to the mat.

Rambo's military training also teaches him to attack from the top down. Get the generals and headquarters (i.e., Mickey) first, leaving the troops (i.e., Rocky) without direction. Rambo will carefully maneuver himself over to Mickey. A quick jab to Mickey's head would be too obvious (plus it would only make Rocky mad as when Mr. T did it in *Rocky III*), so he'll opt for the clandestine approach to eliminate him instead. With lightning speed, he'll turn his hearing aid up to 10. The sudden rush of loud noises will put Mickey into cardiac arrest, distracting Rocky and making his defeat even easier.

BRIAN: OF COURSE, Rambo made escaping from that cell look easy. That's because it WAS easy. What'd he do there besides knock over a few jelly-filled cops? And even then he snuck up on most of them. Much like John McClane, Rambo's good at hiding and striking against weak opponents, but in the open against a real opponent, he's unproven. And comparing Hulk Hogan to Rambo is ludicrous. Hulk had a foot and seventy-five pounds on the diminutive Rocky. Rambo will have no such size advantage here.

Let's look at motivation. Who's going to walk into the ring with something to prove? Not Rambo, of course. It's been well established that he does nothing unless provoked. "I just wanted to get something to eat. They drew First Blood™." (That's how they got the name of the movies, there, Steve.) Rocky, however, is still haunted by the ghosts of thirty-seven former friends and mentors who wouldn't have died if he had done something about it, and they won't rest until he is world champion once again. As Rambo stands in stoic silence, Rocky pummels him like a side of beef. This, of course, gives

Rambo his motivation, but it also gives him a blood clot behind each eye.

And let's talk intelligence, Steve. Intelligence and strategy, in addition to brute strength, are very important in Ultimate Fighting. Rambo is beyond dumb. Have you ever looked at the names of his movies? You've got *First Blood; Rambo: First Blood Part II;* and *Rambo III.* Am I the only one that has a problem with this? The man can't even count properly! True, Rocky is no Rhodes Scholar™, but we have absolute proof that he can count to at least V!

After Dredd starts the fight, the cheers of the crowd flash Rambo back to the taunts of enemy soldiers in Vietnam. After an exhilarating gulp of Lipton Brisk, Rocky steps over and puts an end to the Rambo series for good. Now, if only *Rocky VI* can be stopped . . .

STEVE: I think you *are* the only one who has a problem with the counting. Let me try and explain it to you, at a nice simple level so I don't confuse you. Now the first movie is called *First Blood.* Simple enough, right? The second movie would therefore have the title of the first movie (*First Blood*) along with a "II" in there. Yep! It's there! They've even added a little extra to make it more enticing. They've even equated *First Blood* to *Rambo.* Are you with me so far? Now the third movie in the sequel would have a *III* in there. Whaddya know! It follows nicely, and even has a nice ring to it. Granted, by only going to III, it's obviously not as popular as Rocky. However, no one ever said that being popular and winning Ultimate Fighting Championships are related.

And hey, if you want to talk hauntings, Rambo has Rocky beat handily. Oh no! They killed a grouchy old man posing as Rocky's trainer, riding on his coattails and trying to get some money before he croaks. Gosh, that sure is motivation. Rambo can easily beat this sappy ploy. What about all his fallen comrades in Vietnam who were killed in front of him by Vietnamese torturers? After the first punch lands on Rambo, he'll have a brief (he'll retain awareness of his surroundings, of course) but vivid flashback to being captured as a prisoner of war. We've seen what effect that can have on him. He won't need any motivation after that. In seconds he'll turn into a vicious Fighting Machine™. Rocky will be pulp in about ten seconds. Abandon hope, all ye who enter the ring!

THE OUTCOME

Rambo (60%) knocks out Rocky (40%).

THE PEANUT GALLERY™

After the contestants are announced, the bell rings and the fight is under way. Sadly, years of exposure to automatic weapons fire and devastating explosions have left Rambo completely deaf. He is still ranting incoherently and making incomprehensible threats to the officials when Rocky makes his move.

Years of sparring against sides of beef have toughened Rocky's hands and given him an awesome jab. Of course, they have also given him Mad Cow Disease™. Rocky's bloodshot, bleary Eye of the Tiger™ falls on Rambo. Rocky lowers his head, bellows, and charges toward Rambo's abdomen.

The collision between an irresistible force (Rocky's gigantic cranium) and an immovable object (Rambo's ripped abs), creates a Rift in the Time-Space Continuum™, propelling both fighters to Bizarro World™. Supreme Court Justice O.J. Simpson awards Rambo the Nobel Peace Prize, and Rocky is appointed Director of the Pauly Shore Institute for Advanced Technological Studies.

—Dr. Dave

Since there have been five Rocky movies to three Rambo movies, the five Rockys (Rockies?) will outnumber and beat the three Rambos (Ramboes?).

However, using that logic a Terminator vs. Conan battle would result in a draw—as there are, as I recall, two of each—even though the terminators are far superior to the Conans. But the good news is that they could beat the boogers out of the one and only Kindergarten Cop.

Then, of course, there is the small problem of the Brady Bunch. Actually, the large problem of the Brady Bunch. With the two movies of the family of eight, there would be a total of sixteen of them. Except you have to add in Alice, making it eighteen. Oh, and Sam, the butcher, is "like family," making the total twenty. Does this scare anyone else?

Just think of all the Captain Kirks running around with all the *Star Trek* movies! Everywhere you turn: Kirk!

Then there is the *Batman* series of movies. Four movies. Three different Batmans. Three similarly different Bruce Waynes. Yet no one in Gotham is suspicious.

And don't get me started on the travesty of all those "Hey, Vern!" guys roaming our fair streets. THAT JUST AIN'T RIGHT! STOP THE MADNESS!!! NO MORE SEQUELS!!! IT'S OUR ONLY CHANCE FOR SURVIVAL!!!!

Anywho, I predict Rocky will win by a score of 5–3.

Now, if you'll excuse me, I'm off to Barnes & Noble to reserve my copy of *Grudge Match II: The Sports Edition*.

—Mark Wentz (Rochester, Minnesota)

The Grudge Match™ Panel™

Due to its modest beginnings, the Grudge Match had precious little material from its earliest matches. In order to enhance the Grudge Match Book Experience (and in order to provide even more book-only material for marketability), Steve & Brian solicited the services of the funniest and most consistent Grudge Match fans. These chosen few were allowed to send in new, fresh thoughts on several Classic Grudges™. The best of these responses have been reproduced exclusively in this book. In addition to these new responses, you will see their names and handles peppered throughout all of the matches.

Paul "HotBranch!" Branchaud (http://www.pubnix.net/~paulb) is a Montreal-based technical writer and a rabid fan of the Grudge Match since its inception. He would rather get paid for what he loves to do: creative writing, hockey, reading, and spending time with family, friends, and Murray, his dog. His contributions are dedicated to Helen and the memory of his mother.

Paul Golba is a computer jock and recent MBA graduate from northern New Jersey. The Grudge Match unleashed his repressed creative abilities and provided an outlet for a life-time of obscure information. The world may never recover!

Jeff "jeff" Barton (jgb@earthling.net) is an electrical engineer living in Vancouver, Washington. In his next life he plans to be a cult leader, or a supermodel, or a televangelist.

David "Dave C." Christianson was born into a Betamax family. Despite this he has received degrees from the University of Chicago and University of Washington, can hold a steady job, and is able to carry on limited conversations.

Brendan W. Guy (BGuy@vvm.com) is your typical bisexual, atheist Republican, currently studying history and political science at Texas A&M. His eventual goals are the usual: marry Anka Radakovich, conquer the world, and achieve godhood, but he'll probably settle for going into criminal law.

John "Thinkmaster General" Hnatyshyn (jgh@magma.ca) is a fictional character. It is said that he exists in the illusory city of Ottawa in the fantasy country of "Canada." In his chimerical existence, he works in the inconceivable and outrageous vocation of "economist." Those who have claimed to have seen him have said that he carries with him a satchel of gold.

Shane "Call me Shane" Tourtellotte (smt@webspan.net) is a budding science fiction writer living in northern New Jersey (and no, he's not Paul Golba's roommate). Any resemblance to other writers, living or dead, is purely coincidental—and he dares you to prove otherwise.

Joe "Some Dork" Weber (http://web.nmsu.edu/~joweber) is currently an electrical engineering student (pronounced *geek*). He is glad to be part of the Grudge Match as it tends to make up for the lack of college life at New Mexico State University.

Appendix A

NUMEROLOGICAL PROOF THAT BILL GATES IS SATAN

The real name of Bill Gates is William Henry Gates III. Nowadays he is known as Bill Gates the third.

By converting the letters of his current name to the universal ASCII computer standard values and adding his third, you get the following:

B	66
I	73
L	76
L	76
G	71
A	65
T	84
E	69
S	83
+	3
	666

Also note that when converted similarly, the phrases *MS-DOS6.21* and *WINDOWS95* will also add up to 666.

Acknowledgments

First, thanks to Sam Roadman, a fellow graduate student from the chemical engineering department at Cornell University in Ithaca, New York. He was in on the original inane conversations that led to the conception of the Grudge Match, and has also served on several occasions as a guest commentator for the Web page. Thanks to Nate Robinson, also from our department, who lent us much invaluable technical support.

Many other people have also helped us out by serving as guest or extra commentators for our Web page: Jeff Willits and Mike Petrich, both graduate students in our department; James P. Gerace (gerace@pcnet.com) at People's Bank in Fairfield, Connecticut; V. Darren Arcuri of Canada, and Kurt D. Armbruster, also of Canada. Thanks also to Rod "The Bod" Jackson of Jacksonville, Florida, for written contributions to this book. Thanks to Jim Houghton of Ithaca for the caricatures and to Diane and Bill Alcorn of Pittsburgh for the picture of their Rottweiler, Lyka. And kudos to Dan Willis (zeppo65@aol.com), Digital City South Florida, Fort Lauderdale, who designed and donated the WWWF logo for our website after WWF lawyers cracked down on our first one, and to Todd Edmonds of Iron Design in Ithaca for artistic advice. Thanks also to The Panel™, but they have their own page.

Thanks to our advisors, Professor Michael Shuler (Brian) and Professor Paulette Clancy (Steve) for realizing that it's okay for grad students to have hobbies, as long as they do their research. Thanks also to our parents for their support and advice, and especially for allowing us the many long hours of childhood TV watching that made this possible. Thanks to Jeremie for giving us our Big Break™, and to our Blood-Sucking Lawyer™, David, for his helpful and friendly legal counsel. Brian would like to thank his wife, Susan, for always being supportive of "that Grudge Match" (she knew from day one that this would turn into something big).

Steve would also like to thank Brian for his greater initiative in putting this book together. In turn, Brian would like to thank Steve for thinking of the whole idea and letting him on the Gravy Train at the first stop.

Many of the match-up ideas that appear in this book were actually suggested by friends or E-mailed in by our readers. **Rottweiler v. Chihuahuas:** Toshi M. and Scott C., The 305 Club, Cornell University. **John McClane v. Death Star:** Rich Coughlan. **ALF v. E.T.:** Muneer Ahmad(muneer@falcon.cc.ukans.edu), University of Kansas. *Scooby-Doo v. The X-Files:* Kevin Bush. **Ellen Ripley v. Sarah Conner:** George DeMet (demet@palantir.net), Palantir Internet Services, Harshaw, Wisconsin. **Waldo v. Carmen Sandiego (with T-1000):** Chris Denschikoff (Chris@Banick.com, http://www.banick.com/chris). **Andy Taylor v. The Cunninghams:** Dave Ruark and Andy Liimatta. Thanks also to our own Kathryn Hollar for suggesting King Solomon. **RuPaul v. Dennis Rodman:** Sean "Gui" (rhymes with pee) McGuire and Dan Hartnett. **James Bond v. Indiana Jones:** Marc Caron, Paul Golba, Alex Obaza & Paul Gilbert, and King Paul I Korman. **Rocky v. Rambo:** Jay M. King (jking@linfield.edu), Linfield College, Oregon. Unfortunately, a few matches must go uncredited or poorly credited due to some lost files. Both **Forrest Gump v. Rain Man** and **Rush Limbaugh v. Howard Stern** were suggested by two students (Kristin and Matt?) from Knox College, Galesburg, Illinois. **Orville Redenbacher v. Colonel Sanders** and **Poppin' Fresh v. Mr. Peanut** were also suggested by now-unknown readers. Thanks also to the many people who suggested some of the other matches we've used (such as the 1,273 people who suggested **The Brain v. Dogbert**), but who are too numerous to mention here.

Thanks to the following Web surfers for additional contributions: Aaron, Dan, C. Avatar, mib, TCOH, lance, Chip Kramlich, Marcus, Brandt, Jamie, Rachael & Jim and DeVerne.

Finally, we'd like to thank the people who truly made this possible: our Internet viewers. Without their responses and match ideas, even the ones that don't appear in this book, we wouldn't have this book. Additional thanks to those who have donated their material for use in this text. In their honor, we'll be donating a portion of our royalties to charity.